BAREFOOT IN THE CREEK

Also published by
University of Western Australia Press for
the Charles and Joy Staples
South West Region Publications Fund:

A Tribute to the Group Settlers
by P.E.M. Blond

For Their Own Good
by A. Haebich

Dearest Isabella
by P. Joske

Portraits of the South West
by B.K. de Garis

A Guide to Sources for the History of South Western Australia
compiled by Ronald Richards

Jardee: The Mill That Cheated Time
by Doreen Owens

Blacklegs: The Scottish Colliery Strike of 1911
by Bill Latter

Western Australia as it is Today, 1906
by Leopoldo Zunini,
edited and translated by Margot Melia and Richard Bosworth

*Ritualist on a Tricycle: Frederick Goldsmith
Church, Nationalism and Society in Western Australia 1880–1920*
by Colin Holden

 The Charles and Joy Staples South West Region Publications Fund
was established in 1984 on the basis of a generous donation
made to The University of Western Australia by Charles and Joy Staples.

The purpose of the fund was to make the results of research on the
South West region of Western Australia widely available so as to assist the
people of the South West region and those in government and private
organizations concerned with South West projects to appreciate the needs
and possibilities of the region in the widest possible historical perspective.

The fund is administered by a committee whose aims are to make
possible the publication (either by full or part funding), by the University of
Western Australia Press, of scholarly research in any discipline relevant to
the South West region.

BAREFOOT
IN THE
CREEK

A GROUP SETTLEMENT CHILDHOOD
IN MARGARET RIVER

L.C. BURTON

THE CHARLES AND JOY STAPLES
SOUTH WEST REGION PUBLICATIONS FUND

UNIVERSITY OF WESTERN AUSTRALIA PRESS

First published in 1997 by
University of Western Australia Press
Nedlands, Western Australia 6907
for the Charles and Joy Staples
South West Region Publications Fund

Reprinted 1998

National Library of Australia
Cataloguing-in-Publication entry:

Burton, L.C. (Leonard Crowther), 1919–
    Barefoot in the creek: a group settlement childhood in Margaret River.

    ISBN 1 875560 83 1.

    1. Burton, L.C. (Leonard Crowther), 1919–   .—Childhood and
    youth. 2. Margaret River Region (WA)—Social life and
    customs—1901–1945. I. Title. (Series: Staples South
    West Region publication series).

920.71

Produced by Benchmark Publications Management, Melbourne
Consultant editor Amanda Curtin, Curtin Communications, Perth
Designed by Rosalie Okely, Perth
Typeset in 10 pt Novarese Book by Lasertype, Perth
Printed by PK Print, Perth

To honour my parents
and for
my grandchildren,
Jessica, Alistair and Hamish.

And though I hope not hence unscathed to go,
Who conquers me shall find a stubborn foe

LORD BYRON, 'ENGLISH BARDS AND SCOTCH REVIEWERS'

Foreword

ORIGINALLY CONCEIVED AS A BENEFIT for ex-servicemen from the First World War, the Group Settlement Scheme of the 1920s became a grand plan to bring British migrants to Australia's sparsely populated south-west corner, and to make Western Australia self-sufficient in dairy products. It involved small groups of men working together to clear some of the land and build huts; the land was then divided into blocks and apportioned by ballot to members of the group who, with their families, set about turning it into farms. It seemed a sound plan—visionary even—from a distance. However, the hardwood forest that covered much of the land chosen for settlement, the lack of relevant experience of most of the 'groupies', undercapitalization, and the onset of the Great Depression just as some were finding their feet, meant that hard work, poverty and ultimately heartbreak were the lot of most settlers.

Len Burton's parents were among the group settlers and, at the age of seven, he and his two younger sisters accompanied them out from England in 1927. The long journey by sea, train and truck led them at last to a tin shanty in the bush. There was no tank or well; the truck driver laconically indicated that 'the creek is over there'.

This book is the story of the life the Burton family made for themselves on Group 85, 15 kilometres from where the town of Margaret River now stands, but then in deep isolation. It is an absorbing story, well remembered and well written, which describes the difficulties and privations of the period but without bitterness or regret. And it conveys vividly the pleasures and rewards of life in the bush, especially from the point of view of children.

In the end the Burton family were forced off their land by the collapse of butterfat prices, and illness, but they remained in Western Australia. It would be too easy to say that the long-term benefits justified the short-term costs of what was, by any standard, a disastrous bungle. But it is reassuring to find that at least some survivors of the scheme can look back sixty years on with a tolerant and even affectionate eye. This is not just an informative account of group settlement life but in some ways a heartwarming one. I hope it is widely read.

BRIAN DE GARIS
PROFESSOR OF HISTORY, MURDOCH UNIVERSITY

CONTENTS

ACKNOWLEDGMENTS

This book has had a long gestation period. It may not, even now, have been finished were it not for the influence of many people. I want to thank them all:

my family—sisters Margery and Mary, son Stuart and daughter-in-law Rose—for their encouragement;

my friends of early schooldays for their reminders where memory was weak;

the many friends—they know who they are—for their kindly comments and constructive criticisms.

In particular, my thanks to my editor, Amanda Curtin, whose skills have converted a collection of reminiscences into publishable form.

I do not forget Isobel, my wife of forty-six years, whose support has always sustained me but who, sadly, because of her illness, is unable to share in the final stages of this project.

Finally, to you, the reader, my thanks for your interest. In your judgment of my story, of both the life it depicts and the telling of it, may I commend the concluding words of J.B. Priestley's *The Good Companions*:

In this place…perfection is not to be found, neither in man nor in the lot he is offered; least of all in these tales we tell of him, these rambling hints and guesses, these stumbling chronicles of a dream of life.

L.C. BURTON

Photograph page 24 reproduced with the permission of European Library Publishers, Zaltbommel, Netherlands, from Robin Pearson's *West Bromwich in Old Picture Postcards*, 1988 (photograph no. 91).

Photograph page 22 courtesy Battye Library 2890B/18.

Photographs pages 25, 74 and 85 courtesy Mrs Edna Carruthers (nee Clark).

Painting of group cottage, page 108, by Margery Morley (sister).

Other photographs are from the family collection.

PREFACE

THE SOUTH WEST OF WESTERN AUSTRALIA is a small corner of land not much bigger than England. It stretches from Geraldton, about 400 kilometres north of Perth, to Albany, a similar distance to the south. It has been separated from other land masses for millions of years by vast oceans, and from the rest of Australia for aeons, firstly by oceans and later by arid desert formed from the sea-bed of the receding ocean. So isolated was it that it developed its own fauna and, more noticeably, a flora that is unique in the world. This pocket of land, covered with forests of heavy hardwood and assured of an ample and steady rainfall, appeared to be the ideal place for the development of a 'New England': a garden and farm for the future cities that were expected to develop along the coast. In the extreme south-west of this area, in the third decade of the twentieth century, a socio-economic experiment called the Group Settlement Scheme was conceived and developed. Migrants from the 'Old Country' came, bright-eyed and buoyed with hope to clothe the dream with flesh; lured by the deceptive promotion of those whose vision was greater than their understanding of the difficulties involved.

My father and mother left England in 1927 to join the scheme. They persevered until 1932, when my mother's ill health forced them off the land. This account is an attempt to portray, through a revival of childhood memories, their experiences and the experiences of our family in the setting of the Group Settlement Scheme as it was envisaged and practised. Those who seek historical accuracy or chronological precision in these pages will be disappointed. Important as these are for some purposes, they are not the stuff of childhood reminiscences. It is the flavour of our childhood memories that remains with us in our later lives, rather than their exact order or accuracy. It is this flavour, if it is pleasant, for which we would turn back the clock. It is this flavour also that we would have our children and grandchildren share. The opportunities for actually sharing these experiences — the good and the bad — are, in many cases, gone for ever because of changing and differing circumstances. We cannot turn back the clock and so we must be satisfied with these second-hand narratives, even though they can convey but dimly the pleasures and excitements as well as the hardships of pioneering in the bush.

The stimulus to write these reminiscences came from several directions. There was a television documentary I watched, on a family who had settled in the Northcliffe area about 1910. The presenter, in her introduction, referred to them as 'the last of the pioneers'. Perhaps it was because I was so personally involved that my reaction was: 'What about those who came fifteen or twenty years later, under conditions just as harsh?'. Then there was the occasion on which, at the suggestion of a friend, I contacted a researcher who was supposed to be investigating the human aspects of the Group Settlement Scheme. I do not know how much work she had done before I spoke to her, but she had an appalling lack of understanding of the situation of the settlers. Two comments she made during our conversation have remained vividly in my mind as examples of the limitations of historical and social investigation from a remote perspective.

'It was the type of life', she commented, 'that many young people are seeking today when they opt out of city life — simple, beautiful, ideal!'. The similarity is superficial. Pictorial and anecdotal evidence of many communes give the lie to any such comparison. Today's flight to the country is a flight away from the complications of life; that of the early settlers was more a migration to hope. Present-day communes frequently represent a deliberate search for less crowded conditions, often with the backing of resources in the form of realized assets, savings, severance pay or superannuation with which to provide the materials for housing and at least some comforts. On the whole, the settler migrants had few such resources. Theirs was invariably a transplantation from rented housing, reasonable comforts and satisfactory, if insecure, standards of living. They came to a much lower standard of housing and living, frequently ending up in primitive conditions unrelated to their effort and hard work. The poorest of today's seekers for the simple life may bear some similarity to the group settlers, but there is one important difference—both practical and psychological—that sets the two poles apart. Today, there are social security benefits (unemployment and sickness) available to those without work; then, such benefits were much harder to obtain. Engulfed in poverty, with no means of escape, the settlers were people without hope and largely abandoned by the successors of the governments that had set them up.

The second comment of my researcher contact was to the effect that the group settlers were probably better off under group conditions than they were in the English slums from which they came. This is another fallacy regarding the early settlers, which, by unrefuted repetition, has gained credence among people of later generations. The group settlers were, by and large, not the rejects of the English social system. As is only to be expected, there were as many reasons for individuals to migrate as there were migrants. The immigrants, generally, came from the upper-lower and lower-middle classes of English society. As a body, they were intelligent if not highly educated, and were people of character. Among them were retired army officers, teachers, policemen, clerks, farmers, and people with trades and skills of all types. Many had experienced some sort of setback in their lives. Many, caught up in the rigidities of the class system of English society, saw a hope of escape and upward mobility in the promise of this new scheme, which was being publicized with great optimism by the Western Australian government agencies in Britain and supported with unenlightened enthusiasm by the British Colonial Office.

Herein lie my excuses, if any are needed, for this narrative. My parents were involved in the scheme and I have vivid memories, from the age of seven, of their five and a half year struggles and experiences at Margaret River, or rather at a little-known place about 15 kilometres east of the town, now called Osmington but then known simply as Group 85.

L.C. BURTON

Introduction

THE SPECIAL SETTLEMENT SCHEME, which later became known as the Group Settlement Scheme, was the foster child, if not the brain-child, of James Mitchell, the Minister for Lands in the State Government of the time. It was the subject of negotiations between the British Secretary of State for the Colonies, the Australian Commonwealth Government and the Western Australian State Government, in 1921, and was formalized in the Empire Settlement Act 1922.

The aims, as far as the State Government was concerned, were to promote speedy settlement in the State, to open up the South West, and to make the State self-sufficient in dairy products, for which the region was considered to be ideally suited. An incidental objective was to capture a portion of the export market for butter, which played a not insignificant role in Australian and New Zealand exports to the United Kingdom at that time. As far as the Common-wealth was concerned, the scheme was a means of attracting immigrants to the country. For the Imperial Government, the objective was the opposite: to increase the flow of emigrants to the colonies. This was being encouraged as a way of reducing the population of the home country and of honouring the British Government's pledges to returned soldiers of the First World War.

The State was to provide the land and accept a target of 75,000 new United Kingdom immigrants. The Commonwealth was to raise the necessary loans on behalf of the State. The Imperial and Commonwealth Governments agreed to pay two-thirds of the interest payable by the State in respect of those loans, for a period of five years. By that time, it was hoped that the settlers would be self-sufficient and able to take on the burden of interest payments themselves, in addition to the gradual repayment of capital.

The first group was established on 28 March 1921 at Manjimup.

From its inception, the scheme was promoted widely in glowing terms by the three governments. Propaganda was particularly noticeable at the Wembley Exhibition, in London, of 1924–25.

The attraction for the prospective settler was the opportunity to select land that was absolutely free except for a survey fee and incidental charges, which amounted to about $26. They were offered 80 hectares of arable land but, to allow for outcrops of ironstone, most blocks were 90–100 hectares. The survey was usually carried out so as to include a running creek through each block.

In the settlement of the Western Australian bush, it had long been recognized that distance and isolation were problems that many, particularly women, found insurmountable. It was felt the concept of the group — settlement of a number of families together in a defined area, and encouraging them to work as a team — would overcome this obstacle by providing the companionship and support of a small, ready-made community. A group consisted of twelve to fourteen families. Some of the early groups were assembled in England, but other settlers were allocated places as vacancies occurred.

The first arrivals on the group lived in tents. The men usually moved on to the group alone, leaving the women and children in the city or a nearby town, to follow later when more acceptable accommodation was available. Some migrants even left their families at home in Britain until conditions became more settled. When the move was made to the settler's own block, a humpy was erected and the women and children were encouraged to join their menfolk. This relieved the men of cooking, washing and other necessary chores, releasing their energies for the more speedy development of the block.

Initial development of the block was to comprise an area of 10 hectares partly cleared for pasture, and another 2–3 hectares more fully cleared for intensive cultivation. At this stage, the blocks were considered to be self-sufficient and were balloted for. The families then moved out from the camp block to the one they had drawn in the ballot.

Later, boundary fencing was to be erected and a well sunk for water supply. Settlers were to be provided with a cottage, a small dairy and a milking shed. It was anticipated that this degree of development would take up to two and a half years, during which time the group would work together, developing each block in turn, or sometimes working in small teams of three or four spread over a number of blocks.

The settler was to receive a sustenance payment of $6 per week for three months. Then, after gaining experience, he was to work on piecework (payment according to the amount of work done) until the block was deemed self-sufficient. The rate of payment received while on piecework was set such that no more than about $6–8 per week could be realized. Frequently, women and children would work alongside the men in order to supplement the family income. The foreman assessed the rate per hectare and made a 'contract' with the settler to pay that rate for an agreed area, usually 2.5–5 hectares. If, as sometimes happened on heavily timbered or swampy ground, the foreman underestimated the amount of work involved, the settler had what was known as a 'bad contract'. In those circumstances, the help of women and children was essential to produce sustenance-level income. If the settler had capital and chose not to accept the sustenance or piecework payments, the uncollected monies were credited against the costs of development. The value of these payments in today's terms can be gauged from the budget, published at the time for the assistance of new settlers, that appears as Appendix A.

Timber rights were reserved to the Crown and proceeds were credited to the group as a whole. Expenditure that could not be allocated to a specific holding was charged to the group account and divided among the separate blocks when they were finally valued and the debt transferred to the individual settler.

On accepting a position in the group, each man had to agree to certain conditions: to work to the satisfaction of the officer in control (the foreman); to work continuously unless his absence was approved; that he would be paid only for time worked; that there were no fixed hours for certain work such as burning off; and to do his share of this extra work.

These were the minimum initial requirements set by the authorities in the planning of the scheme. The participants soon learned that there was much more besides. Hen runs had to be constructed and the fowls fed and watered daily. Drains had to be dug. Later on, pigsties and runs had to be constructed and haysheds erected. These were only a few of the many time-consuming tasks necessary for opening up virgin bush that were undreamt of by the established farmer of Europe and even now are in danger of being forgotten in Australia by those who are farming developed properties.

The character of individuals was, of course, important, but the key man in the whole scheme was the foreman. As with all activity where men operate in isolated conditions — whether it be a small army unit, a railway gang, or a group of road workers — the quality and experience of the leader on the spot, as distinct from unseen controllers pulling the strings from a distance, made all the difference to the morale of the group. The foreman had to have expert knowledge of the country, methods of clearing, sinking of wells, preparation of pastures, cultivation of vegetable crops, fencing, drainage and a host of other practical day-to-day requirements of the pioneering group. For this, he was paid $12 per week — double the pay of the settler on sustenance and slightly more than a man could earn on piecework if he had a good contract. By and large, the foremen were temperamentally suited to, and qualified by experience for, the job and there were few complaints on that score.

One remove up the hierarchy was the senior foreman, the person to whom the foremen of a whole district were responsible and to whom they could look for advice. In addition to the qualities possessed by the foreman, the senior foreman was expected to have expertise in the care and management of a dairy herd.

As the name implies, the group was the basic functional unit of the Group Settlement Scheme. But it was more than that. It was also the social and support unit for the people in it. Consisting of twelve to fourteen families of disparate backgrounds, abilities and dispositions, and lacking any cohesive force, the group seemed quickly to acquire a character that radiated an individuality of its own. Each was separate geographically and socially, and was usually also in a different state of development from other groups in the vicinity. In some cases, it almost acquired the characteristics of a clan but without the historical links between the constituent families.

The one unifying sentiment of the group, at least in the early stages, was the spirit of hope and, often, adventure with which its members came to this new land. They hoped for a better and more secure future — if not for themselves, then for their children — and had an expectation that although they were pioneering, they would reap some of the benefits of hard work and a bountiful environment.

As the harsh realities of the situation gradually sank in, hope was replaced by a mood of defiance: a force for coherence just as powerful for the group as the previous spirit of hope. At this stage, all who persevered became united against the forces, official and economic, arrayed against them. Quite a number, prescient of the outcome of the venture, or pressured by misfortune or sheer inability to cope with the harsh conditions, gave up as hope diminished, and abandoned their holdings. This culling out process ensured a residual common factor in those who remained: stubbornness. They would beat the bush and everything arrayed against them and prove themselves yet. Later, as the economic depression deepened, the realities of relentless external pressures prevailed. Determination and defiance turned to despair. Finally, when they were faced with utter poverty, despair turned into something worse: desperation. Clothes were exchanged between families as children outgrew them. Homesteads were abandoned, or families, lacking even the fares to the city, stayed on in near degradation, struggling to survive on the bare subsistence yielded by blocks on which all development had ceased.

In general, the settlers were not the 'poor citizens' they were represented to be by some in the latter days of the scheme, when the government was looking for scapegoats for its failure. They were victims of their situation. The setting of a man's life very largely determines the outcome of his endeavours. Valiant deeds, courageous actions or simple persistent effort are not infrequently submerged and rendered ineffective by overwhelming odds. History ascribes importance to victories and defeats in proportion to their impact on the lives of others. But the nature of heroism is not affected by its consequences. The brave person is the one who makes the attempt, not necessarily the one who succeeds in the rescue. Similarly, the manner in which people react to the vicissitudes of life is a surer measure of their mettle and character than the outcome of their endeavours. The numerous setbacks and occasional triumphs of the 'groupies' (as group settlers became known) were, individually, of little historical consequence, but the reaction of the settlers to their gradually deteriorating position reveals that fortitude and stoical persistence that were characteristic of so many early European Australians.

The question of why settlers tolerated the conditions in which they lived may well be asked. It would be pleasing to record that there was some organized resistance and protest, but there were many reasons why this did not happen. Isolation, distance, sheer exhaustion and lack of finance all militated against active cooperative effort and protest. The settlers were, to a greater degree than most of us, prisoners of their time and circumstances, bound to and absorbed in the development of their holdings. A few, no doubt, had the potential to participate in the wider play of farm politics and community affairs, but as a body they had neither the finance nor the surplus energy required. Such isolation from the mainstream of events and political influence always brings a heavy penalty. In this case, as the central energies of State and Commonwealth were concentrated on the deepening Depression and its attendant problems, the settlements were permitted to wither and fade away. Doubtless, there were some in authority who hoped that the problem would disappear completely.

Stories of hardship and unemployment coming from the city, and, in particular, accounts of poverty, dire want and distress coming from America and England, made it clear that the mists of the Depression had settled on the whole world. The settlers were not alone in their suffering. Here at least there were shelter, food from the farm, and distance to hide from the outside world any shame they might feel. In those times, people felt shame at poverty much more keenly than most do today. Whether it was their own fault or not, men felt that they had let their families down. Women were ashamed and too proud to let their relatives know of their position, feeling that they should be doing something about their own destinies. The time for blaming governments for everything had not yet come. The day of protest over anything but the most momentous issues was also in the future. Although far from being unknown, it was generally accepted that vituperation and frenzied demonstration for every piddling cause were unproductive. Reason, logic and respect for the opinions of others, especially of those in authority, were still a force. There was some understanding, however vague, of the fact that the government and the authorities were in the same pickle as everyone else. When disaster strikes, the front-line troops get the bullets, but headquarters are not without their own problems, albeit of a different sort.

The Group Settlement Scheme will go down in the histories of the time. But history is made not only by the visionaries but also by those who put the dreams into effect. Their whole lives, and those of their children, are shaped by more than the outcome of their endeavours: they are shaped by the often unchronicled experiences they encounter along the way.

CHAPTER One

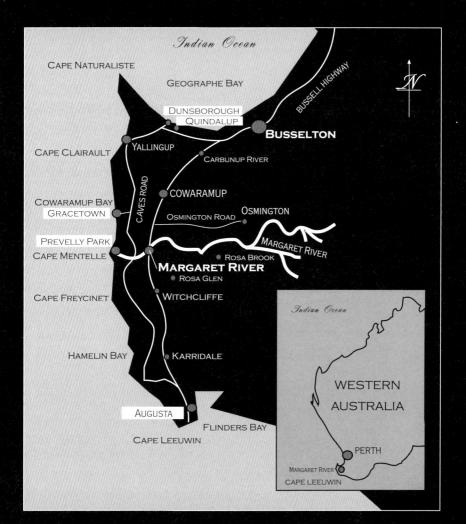

A Migration from Uncertainty to Hope

February 1927; the temperature 42 degrees Celsius in the shade.

Unless one is a resident of those northern locations in Australia where maximum temperatures are over 37 degrees for three months of the year, such heat is nearly unbearable, even to a natural-born Australian. Those living near the coast become acclimatized to the short, sharp bursts of heatwave conditions that characterize the first quarter of the year in the south-west corner of the State. People find them tolerable, knowing that they can usually look forward to some moderation before nightfall, thanks to the gentle southerly breeze off the sea—the Fremantle Doctor, as it is known locally. Experience also tells them that these conditions are unlikely to last more than two or three days, and thus is born an optimistic stoicism.

Not so with my mother, Florrie, who had landed with my father, Bert, and three children the previous day from the RMS *Otranto*. She had no way of knowing about the temporary nature of such heatwaves, nor about the prospects of relief towards the end of the day. The contrast with the bitter cold of the English winter from which she had just been transplanted gave the scorching heat even greater impact. She attempted to escape from the oppressiveness of the weatherboard lodging house in South Fremantle, where we had rented rooms, to the shade of the grapevines outside. These gave the area under the pergola that supported them a deceptively cool appearance. But the heat of the easterlies, coupled with the aggression of the ubiquitous flies, soon forced her back to the shelter of the oven that the iron-roofed cottage had become.

An even more immediate source of discomfort and actual pain was the carbuncle on the back of her neck which, with the help of

Mrs Clarke, the landlady, she had just finished bathing and dressing. It had appeared tentatively at Colombo and had gradually increased in size during the nine-day journey to Fremantle. At the end of the voyage, the pain had become so intense that she was afraid to turn her neck. The tension produced by these restrictions and the rigidity of her posture had brought on a throbbing headache that became worse as each day wore on. She had sought medical attention immediately on landing at Fremantle, the ship's doctor having been unable to do more than recommend hot poultices. The carbuncle had been lanced the previous day, but although this had brought some immediate relief, the wound had not healed enough for her to resume her motherly responsibilities. Her condition precluded any thought of our commencing the overland portion of the long journey to our ultimate destination in the vicinity of Margaret River, about 300 kilometres south of Fremantle.

'When can we go, doctor?', my mother had asked the previous day.

'Where are you going to, Mrs Burton?', the doctor questioned.

'To Group 85.'

'And where is that, exactly?'

'Near Margaret River, south of Busselton; I don't know exactly, but that is what we have been told.'

'Oh yes, I know the area vaguely. There is a doctor in Margaret River, a Dr Rigby, but I'm afraid we shall have to keep you here for another week or so.'

My mother's face showed disappointment and concern. 'We were hoping that we could get on our way. They are expecting us down there and we are, of course, being involved in unexpected expense in staying up here.'

'Yes, I understand. I'm sorry, Mrs Burton; however, it would be unwise for you to go down there until the incision has begun to heal.' He paused, hesitant to alarm her, but eventually, thinking better of his reluctance, continued, 'I have a little knowledge of conditions on the group settlements. Hygiene is apt to be somewhat primitive and, at this time of the year, water is likely to be scarce. In my view, you must not go down until the risk of reinfection is past and until you can manage the dressings on your own.'

There was nothing else for it but to stay. So here she was, awaiting the return of my father with us children from the beach at South Fremantle. He had taken us there to amuse us while Mother attended to the dressing and tried—unsuccessfully, as it turned out, because of the fierce heat—to catch up on some of the sleep lost through pain over the previous few nights.

For my mother, a deeper ache than the discomfort of the unaccustomed heat and the pain of the carbuncle was the sense of separation from loved ones left behind in England. This was more acute than usual now that she was alone, her mind free to wander. Like that of many English women, my mother's world had been the world that existed within a few miles of where she had spent the first thirty-seven years of her life, in the vicinity of the small town of Great Bridge in the English Midlands. She was not completely ignorant of the world beyond. An odd acquaintance or two had moved out from the narrow circle and gone to more distant parts, two of them at least to Western Australia. From letters, occasionally from experiences related during a return visit from someone she knew, from a lecture by a missionary on home leave, or from a travel book, information about distant parts was fed into and stored in an avidly enquiring mind. One close unmarried friend, who had emigrated to Western Australia twelve months earlier, wrote regularly and her letters had brought forth much information about the land that was to become my mother's future home. But apart from an occasional day excursion to the beach or the country, she had no personal experience of the world beyond her immediate vicinity. Prior to coming to Western Australia, her farthest venture had been an extended stay of over twelve months at Middlesborough, whence she had gone as a bride to be with her soldier husband.

This deep inner ache, this dull longing for reunion with loved ones, was perhaps more insidious than the external discomforts and experiences that had to be met and overcome. And it was more potentially damaging to health and morale, because it had to be suppressed. She was determined to keep it hidden from my father and us children: he had enough worries of his own and there was no need to burden us with a sentimental attachment to a past to which there was little possibility of return. She was determined not to become a whinger, a term with which she was as yet unfamiliar, but the antidote to which was epitomized in the Englishman's 'stiff upper lip'. She was a woman in what was then a man's world, but she had made up her mind to maintain, at least outwardly, a courageous attitude.

The separation from loved ones and familiar things, and the isolation of the Australian bush—which is impossible to visualize for people born and bred in the city—were to be the stumbling blocks on which the hopes of many English couples foundered. They were not to emerge as the overt conquerors of my mother's fortitude, but who can tell how much their persistent, secret niggling contributed to the final outcome?

After a fretful hour or so in the heat, my mother went slowly to the gate to welcome us from the beach. There were three children: my two sisters, Margery aged five and Mary aged two, and me, aged seven. Both of the girls were to have their next birthday within the month. The responsibility my parents had assumed was daunting

The author, with sisters Margery and Mary, December 1926, just before migrating.

and, as yet unknown to them, the conditions and prospects towards which they were headed were fearsome. However, as was the case with so many who migrated in that decade, they had ventured out in faith and hope. Unlike many who came after in the 1930s and 1940s, they were not driven by persecution or fear. However, there was understandable apprehension about the future. They came mainly for the sake of us children and they drew confidence from their own good intentions.

My father was a man of medium height and a slight but wiry frame. He had dark, curly hair, and was clean-shaven except for a moustache that he sported in his later years. His face had no striking or strongly distinguishing features, but he had a kindly countenance and an optimistic twist to the lips. There was a wrinkling at the outer corners of his eyes, which were enlivened by an almost permanent twinkle betraying an underlying sense of harmless devilry and humour. My mother knew him well, and it was only when this twinkle went out and he gazed at her or into the distance with listless and unseeing eyes that she sensed his rare descent into despondency or despair. My mother had married him twelve years earlier, against the advice of other members of her

Bertie Crowther Burton, c. 1915, and Florrie Burton, aged twenty-five, 1914.

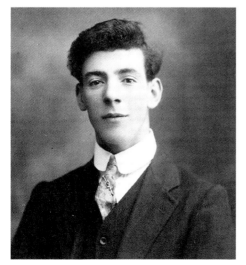

family. He had no prospects, they had said, being only a salesman. He worked first for a firm of produce merchants, Finchers, and later with Powells, a confectionery wholesaler. She had been attracted by his liveliness and mischievous sense of fun—a perfect foil and complement to her own serious and practical outlook. My mother's more serious characteristics were accompanied by a vivacious and strongly independent streak, so she, in turn, supplied some of the missing traits of my father's makeup. They were both fond of cycling, and no matter how careworn or battered by circumstances my mother became in later days, my father always remembered her fresh open smile, and her soft, light brown, waist-length tresses trailing behind her as they went on their weekend cycling tours together. When, in the second year of her stay in Australia, she decided to have her hair shortened, the better to cope with the hot climate and not out of line with the bobbed fashion that was 'in' at the time, there were bitter tears on the part of my mother and protests from my father. Throughout their lives, she was his Florrie and he her Bert and they were to travel together in uncomplicated mutual trust to the end of their days. There was no possessiveness in their relationship; merely a sense of belonging that gave to each of them strength and comfort.

A dim flickering of the idea that was to alter the course of their lives so drastically had first surfaced about eighteen months before their arrival in Fremantle. My father had been to London to see the Wembley Exhibition, which had been advertised widely in all the English newspapers. He seldom did things on his own, much preferring a family outing or picnic on the few national holidays of that time. When he first mentioned the exhibition to my mother, she had said, 'You go on your own, Bert. I don't really want to go and you could get around and see so much more without the children to bother about.'

So, after some demurring, he had gone, setting off by train before dawn and returning after midnight. He had visited the Western Australian pavilion, which at that time was extolling with attractive pamphlets and glowing praise the Group Settlement Scheme in the

South West of the State. 'A Farm of Your Own' was the message. Besides having the support of the Imperial, Commonwealth and State Governments, the scheme had been commented on favourably by the Amery Commission, which had been set up to investigate it. The commission reported that Western Australia was 'the land of sunshine and golden opportunity'. It was no 'bed of roses', as one settler reported to the commission, but most people viewed the scheme optimistically; many considered it the way to independence and eventual prosperity for the enterprising migrant without capital but who was willing to work hard. In fairness, it must be remembered that this report was written before the onset of the Great Depression and the appearance of the economic factors that undermined the scheme. My father brought the pamphlets home and broached the subject gingerly with my mother. 'What do you think about going to Australia?'

This first tentative question brought forth an instinctive, semi-rejecting retort of a surprised and basically contented housewife and mother. 'Australia! What do we want to go to Australia for?'

They went through the pros and cons of the idea together over the course of the next few weeks. There was the insecurity of my father's position with a sole-trader employer who was getting older and obviously less enthusiastic for the business. The business itself was somewhat precarious and there were already signs of alternative distribution methods appearing in the confectionery industry: a change away from wholesaling to direct distribution from manufacturers to retailers. My father knew that if business contracted, he, as the only employee, would have to go and that his employer could carry on alone for some time without a full-time employee to provide for. He was correct in his assessment of the situation: his employer did not replace him when he left. My father also knew that, whether he was fired or not, there were no prospects of any material progress for himself as a wage-earner in the rigid, settled society of England. There was evidence enough of that in the hundreds of labourers and artisans living colourless lives around him. They were all dependent on the steelworks, pottery works or other small and medium-sized industries that were typical of the 'Black Country', as the Midlands area was called locally. Only the unscrupulous and the adventurous were ever able to break out of the vice-like grip in which the system held them. Even those in the employer class were slowly gravitating downwards through the social strata, their factories becoming ramshackle and maintenance being neglected as the uncertainties of their future became more and more apparent.

Already there were isolated instances of unemployment. This troubled my mother and father deeply, as the hopelessness of a victim's position was brought home to them on more than one occasion when unemployment struck those living in the same street. Although devoid of any logical basis for their reasoning, they sensed that there was a change in the air, and that for them it was unlikely to bring better things. It is surprising how frequently this instinctive sense of the lowest common denominator in the economic system can precede that of the social historian, and outstrip the analytical tools of the economist and the accountant, whose forecasting records are notoriously poor. The pity is that for the ordinary employee, there is often no way out. But my father and mother saw a possibility of escape.

The argument that proved most compelling in the end focused on the prospects a move to Australia would hold for us children. In England, without remarkably good fortune or unforeseeable brilliance, we were faced with drudgery and unrewarding labour and effort. In Australia, there was hope of independence and better things. There is no doubt that the pamphlets that my father had been given conjured up visions of the rolling countryside of the English counties and, to the townsman at least, the blissful aspects of a transported rural England.

So it was that in the end they applied, with ambivalent feelings, to the Australian authorities, half hoping that they would be rejected. When their application was accepted, they announced their decision to their relatives and friends and commenced the uprooting process. Too proud to accept an assisted passage, my father paid our own second-class fares, and earmarked an amount for return fares and the retracing of steps if the venture should prove a failure.

A limited amount of luggage could be taken, and choices had to be made. All the large furniture and items like the sewing machine and the piano went to relatives, friends and neighbours at ridiculously low prices. Lists of desirable items for our new life were obtained from the Australian authorities. Recommended tools were acquired, together with a few texts on farming and a plentiful supply of good clothing. Household linen, cutlery and ornaments of sentimental value were carefully packed away. There were two large cases. Another, slightly smaller, containing lighter clothing for the tropics and the summer to which we were headed, was marked 'Wanted on Voyage'. This box was stowed separately in the hold of the ship and made available to us once a week on the outward voyage. There were a tool box, a cabin trunk and several suitcases — so stoutly constructed and of such durable materials that they were put to use for many years after the journey. After a round of parties and farewells with family, we embarked in January 1927 on the RMS *Otranto*. In accordance with the precise scheduling of the Royal Mail Steamers of the time, we arrived at Fremantle exactly twenty-eight days later.

After we had spent eight days in South Fremantle, the doctor pronounced my mother fit to travel. There followed a final round of shopping to purchase items that had been recommended by members of the Migrants Welcoming Committee of the Congregational Church, who had met us on our arrival and eased our immediate problems tremendously by their local knowledge. Such things as a household lamp, hurricane lanterns, a Beatrice stove, as well as a first-aid kit, proved to be practical additions to our small accumulation of possessions.

Travelling southwards on the South West railway, we had our first glimpses of the vast, sparsely inhabited countryside into which we were to be absorbed. The transition from town to country was gradual—no sudden burst from city to countryside as is frequently met with in England. First, we passed along the foothills of the Darling Range at Armadale, where there were small dairy herds and orchards. Beyond Armadale, there were wider grazing lands and dairy farms interspersed with much larger belts of undeveloped bushland. The mixed goods and passenger train—known as the 'Midnight Horror'—had left Perth in the late evening and so these glimpses were but hazy impressions caught through bright moonlight. The harshness of the dry, parched summer landscape was softened by the moonlight, and the night travel heightened the sense of adventure into the unknown. Sleep for the adults was difficult and fitful owing to the frequent stops for shunting at the stations along the route.

We arrived at Bunbury just after dawn, and at Busselton at around 7.00 a.m. Beyond Busselton, the bush became the norm, with only the occasional glimpse of a settler's farm. Most of the holdings lined the track, euphemistically called the main road, that ran parallel to, but some distance from, the railway line; the line itself ran through timber country. We passed the tiny settlements of Metricup and Cowaramup, which, although boasting a railway siding, were some distance from the railway track. In any case, they were but small clusters of timber buildings comprising one or two shops, a post office and bank agency, a school, and the odd home of a railway or other government worker. The cleared, settled land was naturally more intensive near these small centres, gradually thinning out to more outlying blocks, which were some 15 or 20 kilometres away from the place named on the envelope addressed from Britain or other European homelands. In the minds of relatives left behind, these places with such strange names were most probably envisaged romantically as a type of English village, but in reality they bore not the slightest resemblance to those rural hamlets of the old world.

The train finally disgorged us at Margaret River, which today is a small but progressive and thriving country town well known for its fine wines. Even then, it was a centre considerably larger than any of the other settlements passed en route from Busselton. We purchased our essential furniture here: a double bed with folding legs, a deal kitchen table, kitchen chairs and a tin bath. My family had to learn to live without access to shops, and a stock of food was acquired under the guidance of W.H. Samworth, a storekeeper in the town, who always had my father's respect and full confidence. The hired carrier with an old but reliable Ford truck had, under my father's scrutiny, loaded up boxes and trunks from the train. With the recently purchased stores and paraphernalia loaded, we clambered aboard and were off on the final leg of our migratory journey to a future we could not, as yet, begin to comprehend.

g chilly mornings & nights.
- some of it is hard but he
were amongst so much work
ettlement which had been
land is well cleared & our
ack which will soon be a
rside place fifteen miles away
ing concern & are the starting
a master carpenter & to live
id when he came out 42
like these settlements. There are
tinually being made & the

Beginnings

THE DEEPENING SHOCK of the final part of the journey laid a chilling hand on the hearts and minds of my parents. Being city-dwellers, they were used to houses crammed together in the Midlands; houses separated only by a narrow street or alleyway. On the migrant ship, they were herded together into cramped cabins that groaned and almost burst under their quota of four to six persons. And now this! Twenty-five kilometres or more of sparsely scattered clearings — they could not yet be called farmlets, let alone farms — interspersed with increasing stretches of menacing and foreboding bush. Mary slept on in ignorant bliss. To Margery and me, it was an adventure. But to my parents, unaware of what awaited them at their final destination, every kilometre, every bend in the track, every bump — and there were many of them, for the track was rough — led deeper into isolation and brought feelings of unspoken trepidation.

The first part of the gravel road from Margaret River, although as yet without bitumen, was firm and graded. The last 10-kilometre stretch was no more than a bush track. The scarfs of the surveyors' axes were still freshly visible on the trees at the track's edge. In mid-February, with no rain having fallen for over three months, the surface was covered with a fine dust pounded under the hooves of horses and the steel-clad wheels of the settlers' spring carts. The cloud of dust trailing behind the truck carrying us was like a comet's tail, which overtook the vehicle as it slowed down to navigate some fallen tree or a particularly bad stretch of road. The semi-vacuum created by the truck's forward movement sucked in the dust whenever the vehicle slowed down, covering Father, Margery and me, and the goods loaded in the back, with a fine powder.

The tyres of the truck followed the ruts of the carts and vehicles that had passed that way before. Between the vehicle tracks was a third depressed, rutted track made by the hooves of horses as they padded along between the shafts of the carts. The further one progressed, the less distinctive these depressions became, because of the less frequent use of the trail. Towards the end of the journey, there were only the scarfed trees to indicate the route as the faint track twisted and turned around obstacles and fallen trees. In the gullies formed by the creek beds, now mostly dry although a few were moist or had a stagnant pool in the centre of the course, vehicles bumped and jarred their way over logs that had been placed side by side to form a corduroy crossing. Invariably, at either end of these corduroy sections there were stretches of churned up ground where the winter run-off along the ruts in the track had met the already overflowing creeks, and formed a morass. These winter quagmires were now caked hard by the heat of the summer sun. Later, we would traverse the same tracks in a spring cart, driving through the pelting rain with the narrow wheels of the cart sunk up

Section of the road from Margaret River to Group 17. This road led to Group 85 about 10 kilometres further on.
(Courtesy Battye Library 2890B/18)

to its axle and the horse slipping and sliding, sometimes with its belly almost touching the mud. But for now, we had only the relatively minor inconveniences of heat and dust.

Once, during the trip, the wheels of the truck ran over a thick bough lying on the track, tossing it up against the floorboards of the cab with such force that the boards burst upwards from their setting. The driver nonchalantly stopped the truck. Presumably in deference to the presence of my mother, he refrained from the Australian expletive appropriate to such an occurrence, cleared away the bough, which had become jammed under the cab, and nailed the boards back into place. Here my mother had her first exposure to the Australian vernacular. 'She's Jake' was his reassuring but puzzling comment as the truck moved forward again.

Finally, after little more than an hour, we emerged out of the bush into a small clearing. 'Here we are', said the driver, dismounting and signalling the others to follow. 'Here' was a low corrugated-iron shanty: a rough, crude shed that, as we learned later, the settlers called a humpy. The driver deposited his load of humanity and goods outside the shack with almost indecent haste. It was as though he wished to get away from the place before my mother and father could confer and call the whole thing off. And so, as the throb of the engine blended into the silence of the bush, my parents were left to contemplate the situation and survey the surroundings in which they found themselves.

Their attention first settled on the humpy. The walls consisted of sheets of corrugated iron 1.8 metres long, overlapped at the edges and fastened to a framework of unsawn bush timber. This framework was formed of solid bush saplings sunk into the ground at the corners, with less stout posts at various intervals. Onto these were nailed struts and cross-pieces. The iron was fixed with the use of as few nails as possible so that it could be used again after the structure, which was intended to be a temporary one, was demolished. The single entrance—a gap between the corrugated-iron sheets—was surrounded by a wooden frame, whose purpose was more a protection from the sharp edges of the iron than it was structural.

From the top of this hung a piece of hessian: the door. The roof, also of corrugated iron, sloping slightly to afford a run-off for water, was kept in place by heavy logs and boulders. The roofing iron projected from all sides, providing gutterless eaves from which winter rain gushed or dripped on to the soil beneath. Sand was scooped up against the outside of the walls, and primitive flashing was provided where the iron wall met the roof.

Inside, the structure was divided so that about a third of its area formed the kitchen and living area. A doorless gap in the dividing partition provided an entrance to the larger area, which was again divided by a hessian partition to form two areas for sleeping accommodation. There was no flooring; just compacted gravel and sand. A few loose boards were scattered around to provide a buffer from the raw earth, but as these became repositories for ants, centipedes and scorpions, they were a constant source of fear for us children and of anxiety for my mother. She never came to terms with the crawling things of the bush which, although not lethal (except for the rare tiger snake), were capable of inflicting painful stings or troublesome itches. An iron Metters stove jutted out from the

From this…

Fisher Street, Great Bridge, England, where the family lived just before migrating to Australia. Their house is the one on the corner (with advertisements on the wall), to the left of the shop (middle section of the block of three).
(Courtesy European Library Publishers, Zaltbommel, Netherlands)

kitchen into a roughly formed chimney. This was the extent of the amenities in the tiny, crude shelter. Almost without ventilation except for the many gaps between the overlapping iron sheets and spaces in the flashing, it was unbearably hot in the daytime. Fortunately, it cooled down quickly at night to provide a reasonable atmosphere for sleeping.

We did not unpack more than the essentials at this spot. My parents' shock at the primitive conditions paralysed them on the first day, and a visit from the foreman the next day held out the promise that a move to the 'camp block', nearer to the town and within sight of a neighbour, was imminent. The foreman was a kindly man, and I can only assume that he could sense the effect that living on this, the most isolated block on the group, would have on my parents. A less generous version of his motives may be that he knew the settler on the camp block was moving out and he wanted

...to this

A neighbour's humpy, similar to the one in which the family lived for a few months on arrival at the group.
(Courtesy Mrs E. Carruthers)

someone to look after the stable of group horses there. As it turned out, we only stayed at this first block for a month — long enough to introduce us to pioneering of the most primitive kind.

Our first problem was water. There was no tank and no well. Except for a perfunctory indication from the driver of the truck before he left us that 'The creek is over there', there was no sign of a water supply. The presence of a creek would have been obvious to anyone familiar with the Australian bush, but the gradual slope of the land to form a gully and the wide strip of thick ti-tree bushes meant nothing to the uninitiated urban dweller that my father was. Creek bed there may have been, but it was the end of summer, and water had to be searched for. Perpetual streams are seldom to be found in the Australian bush, and the exact location of water along a creek bed was a matter for local knowledge rather than a search by an inexperienced 'new chum'.

The problem was solved very quickly by a visit from the daughter of a neighbour, who had ridden over to welcome the newcomers generally, and to show us where our water source was located. The soak, which we had to share with the denizens of the bush, was merely a shallow depression fed by a trickle of water from a spring. Bright new buckets were brought out for the first time; saucepans and every conceivable container were filled. Experience soon showed that the muddy bottom of the soak was easily disturbed, and the whole pool became muddied if the larger containers were dipped in carelessly. So we adopted the practice of using a small cup or dipper to scoop the water out of the hole to fill the larger containers, the latter being used for water not required immediately. The contents were allowed to settle overnight, and the clear water was drained off the next day for use. As the reserve water in the soak soon became exhausted, we had to exercise care that our draw-off did not exceed the rate of replenishment from the spring.

The ubiquitous kerosene tin, that versatile utility of the Australian outback, had not yet found its way into our household, but we soon discovered it. The kerosene bucket was made by taking the lid off an empty 20-litre kerosene tin, hammering down the jagged edges, punching two holes in the opposite sides of the tin with a nail, and threading a double piece of thick wire through the holes for a handle. A short hollow tube of wood or rubber piping through which the handle was threaded, or a thick piece of cloth wound round it, would prevent the hand being cut when the improvised bucket, weighing 15 or 20 kilograms, was full. A thorough washing with soapy water or a quick exposure to a flame to remove the remaining traces of kerosene—and a very versatile and easily replaceable utensil was ready for use. It was a much more practical container than the easily chipped enamel buckets we had brought with us. Kerosene came from the suppliers, with tins packed two to a stout pine case. These cases were also adapted to various uses, and many articles of furniture—cupboards, shelving, wardrobes and storage containers of all kinds—were made by inventive settlers.

After locating water, my mother prepared a hasty meal. And so ended the first day: we children drifting off to untroubled sleep; our parents trying to dampen the doubts and misgivings that the rude experiences of the day had reinforced. Only the silent trees that remain in that place—if any do remain—can tell how much of their nourishment came from the tears that flowed that night: tears of disappointment, tears for the loved ones far away, tears for 'home', which, although they did not know it then, they would never see again.

My father and mother were not alone in this. A similar drama unfolded time and time again in that now largely forgotten social experiment in the south-west corner of Western Australia.

When the next day dawned, the bright sunlight not only dispersed the darkness but brightened the gloom of spirit that had prevailed the previous night. We could not yet identify the cacophonous sounds coming from outside. We could hear the 'Ka-ka-ka-r-r-r-r' of the kookaburras. That other bird also named with onomatopoeic exactness, the twenty-eight, added its high-pitched 'Twenty-eight, twenty-eight' to the medley of strange morning calls. The most deceiving was the deep 'Caw, caw, caw' of the crows. A quarrelling flock of these brought the whole family tumbling out from breakfast, thinking the cry was human. It provided a moment of hilarity as we realized that we had all been taken in by those deceptive throaty calls.

The foreman rode over early on horseback and allotted to my father the first of his as yet unfamiliar tasks: to dig a well for the permanent supply of water. The well was located not, as might be expected, close to the site of the future homestead but some distance away, on ground high enough to escape the flooded creek in winter. The whole farm was to be divided into small paddocks so that one portion of the land could be grazed while a crop was growing on another, with a hay crop being grown in winter and spring for summer feed. As far as possible, a portion of the heavy soil near the creek was included in each paddock so that cattle could continue to graze on the subterranean clover that continued green and nutritious for a few weeks after the pasture on the higher reaches of the paddocks had dried off. The well was situated at the corner of a paddock where intersecting fences would later be erected. In this way, in addition to supplying household needs, it would supply water for cattle in each of the adjoining paddocks.

Well boards, already on the site, were used to line the sides of the well to prevent the soil subsiding. These boards, precut to fit snugly into one another and lock into position, determined the dimensions of the well. The first part was deceptively easy, but soon blisters were raised on tender hands and the throw of soil to the top of the deepening hole became harder. Where possible, men worked in pairs; by arrangement, our neighbour came over to help. With already hardened hands, he provided not only physical assistance but know-how. But my father did not shirk. He assisted to the best of his ability, shovelling the soil away from the edge of the well and taking his turn at the bottom. At about 2 metres, a platform was rigged up, covering about a third of the area of the hole. A crude ladder facilitated access. These platforms, repeated at intervals as the well deepened, were used as stagings as the throw became longer. In addition to their primary function, they provided the person at the bottom of the well with a measure of protection from anything dropping from above. As the well became deeper, heavy clay, which had to be prised out centimetre by centimetre with a crowbar, slowed progress. Greater care was also needed for all operations. Well boards had to be lowered and positioned slowly to avoid mishaps. The excavated material had to be handled two or three times as it was transferred from one staging to another. Towards the end, progress was so slow in the cramped conditions that the best result was achieved by using a kerosene bucket to haul the debris up bucketful by bucketful. It was a back-breaking, tiring task for the person who did the hauling. The man at the bottom took shelter from any spilling sand should the lip of the bucket catch on the edge of one of the stagings, or from a falling bucket should a rope break.

The first seepage of water came at about 4 metres. This was encouraging but it made working conditions at the bottom more uncomfortable. Mid-summer was the best time to dig a well, because it eliminated the need for deepening it at a later date, but the summer heat made the task most trying. As the well was deepened, the water seeped in at an ever-increasing flow. The bottom was kept as clear as possible by a drainage hole at one corner, but this meant that, besides the sticky mud, surplus water had to be conveyed to the surface with increasing frequency. When the flow could no longer be contained, and after the rate of flow had been tested a few times, the well was complete. The stagings were removed, a hand-pump installed, and the top of the well covered with stout boarding. A supply of clean potable water was now assured, and despite the haul up to the humpy, we revelled in complete baths for the first time since our arrival, without any fear of diminishing the water supply. The week's work had been well rewarded.

Welcome relief and a respite from the digging was afforded by visits from other neighbours, mostly English, who came to introduce themselves. It was generally known that we would soon be moving to the camp block, so rather than commiserating with us over the conditions on our present site, neighbours gave us encouraging hints that the new block was a much better one. The camp (or group) block was so called because it was the site of the camp established when the first party of settlers arrived to pioneer a new group. New groups were given a number in order of their establishment. This one was known as Group 85 until it was named Osmington in the mid-1930s. The occupier of the camp block attended to the collective needs of the other settlers in the early stages of development. He also cared for the horses, which were common property until they were later allotted to individual settlers. An advantage of this camp block was its situation on the banks of the Margaret River, about 5 kilometres nearer to the town than our original block. It was also slightly less isolated, as the foreman called regularly on his way to visit the more outlying blocks. Although it was somewhat further advanced than the others, nearly 12 hectares having already been cleared, this made little practical difference, as the men were still working as a team clearing the outer blocks to bring them all up to equal levels of development.

My parents did not really know what they were going to, but it was with some relief, after about a month persevering with the primitive, isolated conditions at that original block, that they packed up our belongings once again and moved.

Conditions in the humpy on the new block were no better, but word had come through that teams of carpenters were on their way to erect the permanent group cottages. The prospect of improvement in the near future somehow seemed to make the present conditions more tolerable. The occupier of the camp block had the responsibility of going into town to purchase stores and supplies for the other settlers. Every Monday and Thursday, my father travelled by spring cart the 20 kilometres into Margaret River to collect groceries and mail for the whole group. This took all day. He was always accompanied by our fox terrier, Spot, who used to trot along under the axle of the cart between the wheels. One approached the township through about half a kilometre of thick scrub that pressed

in on the graded, gravel track euphemistically called the main road. A stand of magnificent karri trees had once thrived there, but by the time we arrived, only smaller trees were left. The track was lined on either side with huge stumps, about 2 or 3 metres high, pitted with holes where the loggers had fixed their felling platforms. A herd of brumbies roamed the perimeter of the thicket. They would watch the approach of the cart from a safe distance and crash off through the scrub if the excitable terrier should try to pursue them. The river was crossed by a railed, wooden bridge that had deteriorated considerably through shrinkage and wear. Its loosened planks rattled under the passage of the cart. In the middle of the crossing, the dog would stop and wait in the centre of the bridge. Watching until the cart turned off the main road, he would then return home alone.

The days following these trips to town, Tuesday and Friday, were mostly taken up delivering groceries to the various settlers and collecting orders for the next run. My father was well suited to this particular job. Gregarious and cheerful by nature, he got on well with everyone and attended to their little requests and needs, faithfully carrying out many extra commissions and errands. This meant a great deal to those living in complete isolation without access to shops.

He soon settled down into the new routine. In between his other duties for the group, which took up much of his time, he managed to dig his second well—an experienced hand by this time—to provide water for the new property. Meanwhile, the existence of a large pool in the river on the edge of the property meant that we were able to be more liberal with our usage of water than we had been at the previous location.

After we had been on the camp block for about a month, a team of carpenters arrived to erect our cottage. Although it was only a very modest structure, the cottage brought about a considerable improvement in our living conditions. It was a timber-framed weatherboard cottage of four rooms, with verandahs at the front and rear. We children watched with great interest from a safe and unobtrusive distance as it gradually took shape through the efforts of the small team. They first laid out the stumps to raise the flooring timbers off the ground, capping them with tin to prevent incursions by white ants. Next, the flooring joists were affixed and the framework of the walls and inside partitions laid out on the ground nearby.

The building's appearance was transformed one day when these frames were lifted into position and secured together. The ceiling and roof timbers were then put into place and the corrugated-iron roof nailed on. The outside walls were clad with weatherboard, and the tongue-and-grooved jarrah flooring nailed into position. The lower part of the interior walls was of jarrah panelling; the upper portion and ceilings were Ceilite plasterboard. The Ceilite was fixed on to one side of the interior walls only, which meant that the hairy reverse side of the plasterboard and the supporting frames of some of the interior walls were fully exposed above the panelling. There was an open fireplace in the front room, formed from a galvanized-iron frame and chimney, while a Metters stove set in a similar frame supplied the means of cooking and warmth for the kitchen. A

The group cottage, 1929, into which the family moved from the humpy.

Rear view of the group cottage, just prior to demolition in 1989.

1,000-gallon (4,550-litre) tank collecting run-off from the roof was the basic water supply, supplemented by water from the river in times of scarcity. The tap of the tank was on the back verandah; there was no water laid on in the kitchen. Nor was there a bathroom or a sink. Hot water for ablutions had to be boiled on the stove. Although the cottage was humble and rude, the quality of the timber was excellent and the workmanship good. Maintained with an occasional oiling of the exterior walls, these group cottages were still occupied fifty years later and a few are still standing today.

My parents missed the refinements of the comfortable home they had left behind in England, but made the best of it and never complained or pined in front of us. From their frequent talk around the meal table, however, we did glean the flavour of different and better things that had been their lot in England and which, some day, they hoped would be ours. We learned from their example to be satisfied, which is an invaluable recipe for a happy life as long as it does not lead to lassitude and erosion of reasonable ambition. Our lot was no different from that of those around us, and even that is conducive to a degree of contentment.

However, Mother and Father were determined to conceal the difficulties of their new life in Australia from relatives and friends in England. This—as well as their optimism—can be seen in a letter 'home' written by my mother just three months after our arrival on the group:

…We arrived at Fremantle Feb 8th, stayed a week and came to our settlement Feb 17th. We are getting along alright and so far have no cause to regret coming. None of us have ever been better in health. The climate is lovely. We've had more sunshine up till now than we used to get all the summer in England, but we must expect the rain soon. It is getting chilly mornings and nights. Bert's work is varied and interesting. Some of it is hard but he looks much happier than when we were around so much worry. We were fortunate in getting on a settlement which had been started over three years ago so the land is well cleared and our bungalow is on the main group track which will soon be a made road through to a nice seaside place fifteen miles away. These settlements are quite a growing concern and are the starting of new places. We were talking to a master carpenter who lives in Perth (the capital of WA) [and] he said when he came out 42 years ago parts of that city were like these settlements. There are many miles of railways and roads continually being made and the man who is not at work in WA doesn't want it. We have met many English people but none who wish to return. The children love this life…How are you all getting along? We miss piano very much but we have other advantages so we have to try to forget.

CHAPTER THREE

DEVELOPING THE EMBRYO FARM

THE DUTIES ATTACHED TO THE CAMP BLOCK gradually disappeared. After about six months, the storekeeper in Margaret River extended his weekly run to cover the district. Later, there was the occasional call by an itinerant salesman. There were two regulars: one came fortnightly with fresh vegetables; the other, every three months with materials and cottons. There was also the annual catalogue from Bairds and Boans, from which country people could order goods not readily available in the Margaret River stores. Thus, my father's responsibility for the collection and distribution of groceries came to an end. But not before the passage of a whole winter. Twice a week, he made the 20-kilometre journey into town and return, and twice a week the stores were distributed—making four days of travel a week, often in the driving rain. His only protection was warm clothing, a good mackintosh, and a waterproof groundsheet slung loosely over his body to divert some of the downpour. During these winter trips, the spring cart sometimes became bogged in a creek bed as the horse, slipping and sliding in the mud, failed to keep up sufficient momentum to tackle a rise after emerging from a gully. If only one side were bogged, leverage applied to the spokes of the wheel, to assist the horse, sometimes worked. If both wheels were sunk and first efforts were unsuccessful, the cart had to be unloaded and its contents carried up to drier ground and placed some distance off the road, for safety, in case the horse was diverted after the cart was freed.

My father would have to dig out the oozing mud in front of the wheels, but often the road surface was of near liquid consistency and fresh mud would seep back as fast as it was dug out. Bushes, bark and young saplings were cut and placed in front of the wheels. Then, with encouragement and urging, the horse, struggling and insecure in the mud, would heave and strain in the harness to tug the cart out of the bog. The suction of the clinging mud on the wheels was often so great that two or three attempts had to be made before the cart could be dragged clear. Very occasionally, a local settler, perhaps half a kilometre away along a lonely track, had to be called on to assist, usually with a fresh animal to replace the tired horse in the shafts. It was always heartwarming to see with what ungrudging cheerfulness this help was given, probably as an unspoken acknowledgment of assistance received on some other occasion. Such was the spirit of the time. After the cart was extricated and settled surely on firm ground, the goods would be reloaded and the journey resumed.

When virgin bush was being developed, one of the first tasks was to kill off the larger trees by ringbarking them. This was done to prevent them from denuding the surrounding soil of moisture and nourishment, to the detriment of future crops and pasture. Ringbarking was done in two ways. One way was to cut off the bark in a broad band, about 20–30 centimetres wide, right around the tree. This was the slower method in terms of results, as the sapwood just under the bark on the outer part of the trunk continued to carry moisture up the tree for some time. Not infrequently, the bark would regrow and sustain a modicum of life in the tree through the resulting scar, and the area would have to be gone over again the following year to ensure a complete kill. However, in terms of effort required, it was much quicker than the alternative method: sap ringing. This consisted of chopping a V-shaped cut right through the bark and the white sapwood and into the red wood underneath. The cut was about 4 centimetres wide on the bark and 3–4 centimetres deep. Sap ringing produced a quicker and more effective kill than the other method. A few larger and well-shaped trees were always left on the perimeter of the paddocks, to provide shade for the animals.

The task of ringbarking frequently gave a settler his first opportunity for a thorough exploration of the block, and occasionally he would come upon a spot where, several years before, sleeper-cutters had gone through the bush, selecting and cutting down the best of the trees for sleepers. Such a find always yielded a cartload of excellent dry jarrah chips and cuttings of various sizes for firewood, as the early method of cutting sleepers with axe and adze was very wasteful.

The year following ringbarking, the area had to be retraced, this time knocking off the new growth that always sprang up from the trunk of the tree below the level of the ringbarking. This 'sucker bashing', as it was called, was accomplished by use of a slasher, a cutting instrument at the end of a strong handle.

Another job to be completed early in the development program was the killing off of zamia palms, which grew prolifically throughout the area. If this were not done, cattle would eat the palms and suffer from a staggering disease similar to rickets, brought on by the poison from the plants. Settlers killed zamia palms by stabbing the heart of the palm with a crowbar, thus making a hole in which rainwater would settle and, with the aid of the heat of the sun, rot the pineapple-shaped root below the ground surface. The killing process could be hastened and made more certain by filling the hole with kerosene, but this was too expensive for general application. The crowbar was very heavy and the work tiring, particularly for a young boy, and therefore it was done in short bursts, but I have no doubt now that my assistance saved my father many hours' work.

Fencing was another time-consuming task. With corner survey pegs already in position and paddock subdivisions marked out, the next task was to fence the outer perimeter of the block. First, the line between the survey posts was cleared of all scrub and trees. Then large tree trunks, about 40 centimetres in diameter, were cut and placed in position at every corner, or wherever the fence changed direction. These 'strainers' held the whole structure firm when the wires were tightened.

Fence posts were cut from trees readily available on the block. The prospect of going tree-felling was exciting to a young boy and I usually accompanied my father into the bush on these expeditions.

This was mainly because he knew I liked to go, but it served an additional purpose in that it provided a second person to raise the alarm in the event of an accident in the course of this potentially dangerous operation. After a suitable tree had been selected, the 'belly', a V-shaped wedge, was cut out of the trunk facing the direction in which the tree was intended to fall. The back half of the trunk was then cut, sometimes with the axe, but preferably with a cross-cut saw wielded by two people, as it caused less vibration in the latter stages of the operation, reducing the likelihood of a dead branch being shaken loose. Precautions had to be taken before this was done — usually before the tree was cut at all — to ensure that the surrounds of the tree were cleared of all debris so that the cutters could run to safety when the tree began to fall. Dead branches on the tree to be felled and on trees in the vicinity were always checked. As the centre of the trunk was approached, there would be a gentle creaking, which gradually became louder and more drawn out as the tree began to tilt forward. This was the most dangerous point in the exercise. One had to cut deeply enough so

The author using cross-cut saw, with Margery and Mary, 1927.

as not to leave the tree poised and yet not remain too long in case the tree gave way suddenly or sprang back. Judgment of the correct moment for retreat came with experience. When the tree was emitting its final groans and was clearly falling, the cutters would run as far as possible from the base of the tree, to avoid danger.

After ensuring that there were no dangerous overhead branches on any of the trees that had been brushed in the fall, the cutters would approach the tree for the next stages of the operation — barking, and cutting the tree into suitable lengths for splitting. The bark was removed by hitting it firmly with the back of the axe over most of its surface, after which it could usually be prised off easily. The logs cut from the trunk with the cross-cut saw were then split into triangular fence posts, each face of the post measuring 10–15 centimetres. A well-selected tree — selection being made by a careful examination of the outer bark — would split easily, the post springing up from the log with a 'crack' as the iron wedges were driven home with a steel mallet. Posts from a poorly selected tree, with cross-grains on the outer bark, would have to be prised apart inch by inch.

The posts would then be bored with a brace and bit, making holes for the wires to pass through, then carted to the fence site and positioned at intervals along the fence line. They would be dropped into the post-holes, which had been dug with shovel and crowbar, with the bored holes facing in the correct direction, straightened up and the earth rammed back into position. The fencing wire was then threaded through the holes from the strainer end. The coil of new wire was generally laid out on a crude turntable to facilitate unrolling. The threaded wire was made taut by being pulled with a pair of chains, which were also called strainers. At the end of each chain were specially adapted grips that caught the wires like a vice and prevented them from slipping as they were tightened. The chains were pulled tight by a lever and prevented from recoiling by a clip that locked into the chain after each operation. This could be dangerous, as the grips occasionally slipped: not a few fingers were severed, usually but not always when the operator was careless. The secret was to proceed with extreme caution and ensure that the tension was firmly established before attempting to lock the clip. The second strand of wire from the top was usually a barbed wire strand that was not threaded but fixed on the inside of the post by a length of thin, pliable wire known as tiewire. Finally, wire netting, known as cyclone wire because of its brand name, was fixed to the lower part of the fence. The whole family usually helped with the fencing operation. Even we children could assist by ensuring that the coiled wire unravelled properly at the turntable, by cutting the tiewire into short lengths, by threading these through the holes preparatory to affixing the barbed wire, and by twisting the ties to secure the positioned barbed wire and wire netting.

The work that probably gave most satisfaction was the clearing of the bush itself. It was hard, backbreaking work, but the vision, still bright, of the rolling pastures that would take the place of the bush spurred us on. The low scrub was first knocked over with a slasher or 'grubbed' with a mattock, or 'grubber' as we called it. Small trees had to be taken out by the roots. It was essential that an adequate distance be cleared between the larger trees, to permit the passage of ploughs, cultivators, harrows and harvesting machinery; therefore, where two trees grew close together, one of them would have to be removed. This was a mammoth job. If the tree had a reasonable lean and the path of its fall was clear of other trees, a deep trench would be dug round its base, and the roots cut one by one until the tree fell. The roots on the side towards which the tree was leaning were cut first; the back roots were cut last, to permit the tree to fall safely. If the tree had dead limbs, or was upright, or would be in danger of fouling other trees when it fell, this method could not be used and the tree had to be cut down. The root was allowed to die off and was burned later.

After an area had been cleared and the debris thoroughly dried off, it was burned under controlled conditions, always against the wind. The burn was an exciting event and was usually attended by a few neighbours, to ensure that the fire did not get away. After the flames had died, the remaining timber — and there was always a great deal of it—was dragged by hand or by horse-drawn chains to central points for continued burning. The use of a horse in this way was known as 'snigging'. Invariably, some of the heavy timber lying around was half rotten and thoroughly soaked with moisture—particularly in creek beds and swampland—and a small charge of dynamite would have to be used to fracture it before burning. The fires often required stoking morning and night, to keep the burning logs together. Occasionally, if a fallen log were especially large or water-logged, the fire would require refuelling. The spectacle of a dozen or so huge fires on a pitch black night was captivating—especially the skyward burst of sparks as my father pushed the smouldering logs together with his crowbar on the final round of the night.

The ground on the banks of the creeks was covered with almost impenetrable ti-tree. This had masses of intertwined root systems that had to be grubbed out if anything were to grow. These creek beds were always the hardest areas to clear but, as they consisted of damp, heavy, black soil, they were the most fertile. The pasture grown on these lands was also valuable because it provided extended grazing for cattle during the early summer months, thus conserving hay and silage. In the rush for early development, these difficult areas were usually cleared last, despite their obvious special value. Clearing riparian gullies was also time-consuming, as they were heavily timbered with blackbutt, a particularly hard timber. There were often a great number of fallen trees, long dead and waterlogged, lying in among the thick scrub. Because of the difficulty of clearing creeks and gullies, these areas attracted the highest rate of pay when the settlers moved on to piecework. Apart from the karri country, the bush in the Margaret River area, particularly along the river banks, was among the thickest of the South West forest, but it never attracted a higher rate than $16 per hectare. To clear half a hectare per week to the satisfaction of the foreman, settlers had to work long hours daily and at weekends. And, after all, it was no use skimping on the work, as it was to be their own land.

The next task after the burned area had been properly cleared was ploughing with a single-disc, one-horse, stump-jump plough. This was followed by cultivating, harrowing, seeding, and harrowing again. Seeding machines were supplied, one between every two settlers, but trying to manoeuvre them between the trees and remaining stumps was more trouble than it was worth. The usual practice was for seed and superphosphate to be mixed and placed in the back of a spring cart from which the tailboard had been removed. I would drive the horse in as straight a line as possible across the paddock, while my father sat on the floor at the rear of the cart, with his feet dangling down. He would pick up a handful of the mixture in his hands and throw it across his body, first to the right and then to the left — a job best done in a slight breeze, which helped to scatter the mixture. This was all right while the wind was behind us but on the return leg, with the wind blowing in my father's face, the fine super dust would blow back on the cart, covering us both in a white powder and stinging our eyes. On areas unsuitable for the use of horse and cart, spreading was done on foot, the mixed seed and superphosphate being carried in a hessian bag held by straps slung round the shoulders.

Deep ploughing was not the best method to use on the high ground, with its shallow layer of fertile soil. But this was not generally realized until much later. Another system of clearing came into vogue at a later date, developed by, and named after, an Italian settler named Mazzoletti who lived near Denmark. This method involved a very light clearing of the scrub, a quick fire and a light cultivation. Heavy timber and fallen logs were left and the semi-cleared block was seeded with clover in time to catch the autumn rains. This produced some pasture for the cows at an early date, permitting the more intensively cleared paddocks to be used to grow hay and ensilage for the summer months. Further clearing would be done during the summer after the feed had dried off. Gradually, over a few years, the area would be brought into full production, while in the meantime supporting a small herd.

Next, the blocks had to be drained. Trenches of various depths were dug around the perimeter of the paddocks and also through the middle wherever two inclines happened to meet. A deeper drain was dug along any creek bed, to hasten the flow of winter floodwaters. The aim was to keep the paddocks as dry as possible, because pasture submerged for too long tended to rot. The whole drainage system interlocked and was carefully planned in accordance with practices current at the time. Contour drainage had not yet been introduced, and drains tended to run parallel to the fence lines. Before the deep drain along the creek bed was dug, the thick ti-tree scrub had to be cleared along its route. The drain was then dug the hard way—with mattock and shovel—beginning from the point at which the creek left the property, in case of heavy falls of rain before the job was finished. It had to be done in the summer months when the creek was dry or not flowing strongly. The heat in the middle of the thick scrub was stifling, with mosquitoes, flies and spiders a constant irritation. A crude template was used to ensure that the sides were uniform and the depth constant, and a line was strung to make sure the drain was straight.

In later development work, my father built a pigsty and a pig run, which involved enclosing about a hectare of land with boards split by hand from the forest timber. Good splitting trees, sought in the uncleared portion of the block, were felled and cut into sections. Posts, rails, and jarrah boards about 2–3 centimetres thick were split from the logs in the same manner as were fencing posts. The boards were sunk about 60 centimetres into the ground, so that the pigs could not burrow underneath them, and were fixed by a rail on either side to hold them in position. The rails were fixed to stout posts sunk into the ground at suitable intervals. This provided a very solid fence that the pigs never breached.

The building of a hayshed by my father's own, almost unaided, efforts was quite a feat. First, tall, straight saplings had to be found, from which 6-metre posts were cut, to carry the roof. These posts were usually pulled into position by a horse, with tackle swung over the branch of a nearby tree or from a specially constructed tripod. This operation required at least two men: one to handle the gear at the post end; the other to handle the horse. My father earned some admiration from his neighbour by doing the job himself, with the assistance of my mother instead of a horse — the subject of some joking among friends. He learned the trick from a telegraph linesman who happened to be working in the district. The method was to dig first the hole for the post and then a tapered trench reaching about two-thirds down the hole at one side. A crowbar was placed at the back of the hole opposite the trench. The post was rolled to the trench, its base against the bar. The far end was then lifted and a large wooden box placed underneath. My mother edged the box along the post towards the crowbar as my father lifted the far end, with each lift raising it to a more upright position. Finally, the post reached a near vertical position and slipped down the crowbar into the hole. All that remained was to straighten it up and compact the earth around the base. The roof trusses and galvanized-iron roofing were then fixed in position.

Thus, over a surprisingly few years, the embryo farm was developed out of the virgin bush. While this was progressing, the ordinary day-to-day work around the farm continued and the little herd gradually increased. Few of those who carried out this development by the sweat of their brow reaped the benefit of their labours. Those who came later, purchasing the properties at giveaway prices and developing them for cattle raising, vineyards or other purposes, are seldom aware of the backbreaking methods used in those early pioneering days. The clearing contractor of today, with his bulldozer and heavy machinery, can have little idea of the frenzied effort required to hack a viable area out of the hostile, tenacious bush, with a primitive slasher, mattock and axe. These efforts are described in some detail here because the real significance of the terms 'early settler' and 'pioneer' is likely to be buried with the children of those stout-hearted first-generation migrants of the Group Settlement Scheme.

Of course, it must be acknowledged that the wholesale clearing of pristine forest would not be tolerated today, let alone encouraged as it was then. But the State was young, resources seemingly inexhaustible, and economic imperatives — including the State's need for self-sufficiency — extremely pressing.

Developments affecting the whole community provided diversion and interest, not only for the children but also for the adults, who welcomed any distraction from the isolation.

There was the arrival of Bonola's timber mill, around 1928. The mill employees were mainly single Slav or Italian migrants: hard-working timber-cutters who lived frugally in order to support families in Europe and eventually to bring them, or a bride, out to Australia. The cutters worked over the many tracts of Crown land in the district in succession, cutting out the merchantable timber left by the sleeper-cutters who had gone through a few years earlier. We saw teams of strong horses pulling the whims, massive logs chained to the sturdy frame between the huge wheels. The scars left on the tracks made passage over them more hazardous and bumpy for the spring carts of the settlers, especially in the softer creek bed valleys. Smaller logs were loaded onto drays — solid, stout-framed vehicles without springs — drawn by a team of horses. Where the roads permitted, the smaller logs were loaded onto trucks and secured by steel spikes and chains. These same trucks were used to convey sawn timbers to the railhead.

We watched the teams of horses tugging and straining at their loads as they navigated the bed of the creek that ran through our property. They were encouraged, in a rather frightening way, by a teamster who cracked his rawhide whip with spectacular ferocity. However, I never saw him hit the horses and I remember him telling me once, seeing my concern, that he never did so. Although they were often white with sweaty foam, there was never any sign of blood, which there would certainly have been had the horses been flayed with that cruel whip. We called the teamster 'Gee-Woah-Back-Doll', for that was his constant cry as he restrained the lead horse, Dolly, on the gentle descent to the creek bed and through the slippery bog. On the other side, his urgent 'Giddap Doll' and the fierce cracking of the whip resulted in the whole team heaving and straining at taut harness and chains, to avoid the inertia of a stalled load on the steady, slippery rise.

The other great diversion was the arrival of the road gang. They set up their camp in one of our uncleared paddocks, near the side of the road. The camp consisted of small tents for the single men who formed most of the gang, and some larger tents, each with a fly set-up in front, for the married couples. There was also a large marquee that was used as the dining tent. This last had a rough corrugated-iron shelter at one end to provide dry conditions for the cooks to prepare the meals. Cooking for the whole gang was done by women who probably had been engaged for that purpose, as the rough conditions were unsuitable for married couples generally. If the enticing aromas that emanated from the kitchen and marquee, permeating the cold air of the early mornings and late evenings, were anything to judge by, the men were served appetizing and healthy meals.

Each morning, the men would set out for the working site on foot, straggling along like an unchained convict gang, with their shovels, crowbars, cross-cut saws and other implements stowed on a horse-drawn dray, or, if the dray had gone directly to the gravel pits, carrying their primitive tools on their shoulders. When it rained, most of them wore capes made from empty chaff bags. It was from this gang that we learned the usefulness of this type of cover. Doubled over lengthwise, the corner of the bag provided a pointed, cape-like cover for the head, and the long hessian cloak provided an effective protection for our clothes. The rain seldom penetrated the double layer of hessian and we usually arrived at our destination dry after passing through the heaviest of showers. Our conventional coats kept us warm but became wet through and remained damp for hours unless protected by these rude but effective covers.

The roadworks were as primitive as the implements used to produce them, involving the minimum of work necessary to turn bush tracks into passable all-weather access ways. The bush on both sides of the existing tracks was cleared away. Any verge trees that looked likely to fall across the road were cut down and moved to the side of the road, or burnt. The road was built up in the centre with gravel. Drainage was provided where necessary, and run-offs dug at suitable intervals. In the creek beds, culverts or, where occasion demanded, small bridges were installed to take the main flow of water. The former corduroy approaches were built up with gravel to form a solid all-weather surface, which also provided an effective barrier to the water if the creek became swollen with winter rains, channelling it through the culvert or bridge. Ironstone patches from which gravel was extracted abounded. The gravel was hewn out by mattock and shovelled by hand onto the horse-drawn drays, for transport to the required site. After the gangs had passed on, these gravel pits were to be found every couple of kilometres along the road. After the war, they were levelled by bulldozers to blend in with the surrounding terrain. Today, one would be hard-pressed to recognize where they had been.

One of the road workers—the foreman, I think—had an old motor vehicle. One weekend, he took my father on a fishing expedition to Cowaramup Bay (now Gracetown), about 30 kilometres away. Besides bringing home a bag of herring, which provided a welcome change of diet, my father also brought back a collection of seashells for us children. In those days, the coast along the bay, desolate and seldom visited, abounded with shells of many varieties. I realize now how rare some of those specimens must have been, or would be today, and what pride of place they would have in some enthusiast's collection.

When the walking distance from the camp to the section of the road on which the gang was working became too great, the camp was shifted to another site. The little community of intruders passed out of our ken, the bustle subsided and the peacefulness of the bush reigned once again.

There were no other intrusions as dramatic as the coming of the mill and the road gangs. On one occasion, a lone Aborigine hawking clothes props appeared, slowly trudging up the road. A single prop—merely a slender forked sapling stripped of bark—was on one shoulder, two were on the other, and a small swag hung at his back. Unfortunately for him, we had already made identical props from the plentiful bush saplings, so my mother gave him some food and he went on his way to the next farm.

Then there was the quiet intrusion of the possum hunters, who pitched their tents on our block while they worked the vicinity. From the trappers, we learned how to identify which trees, principally banksias, the possums frequented. We also learned to read the possums' movements by the smoothing of the rough banksia bark as they scaled the same tree night after night and by the traces of fur left behind. And we learned to tell, by their droppings, whether a tree was still frequented or whether it was a dead trail. The trappers collected their catch of possums every morning, skinned them and hung the pelts out to dry in the sun. They shot kangaroo for meat, and it was during their visit, which lasted about a fortnight, that we had our first — and, as far as I remember, our last — taste of kangaroo steak and kangaroo tail soup.

There was a period when it seemed we were constantly being exposed to these and other new experiences, but gradually, almost imperceptibly, our routine became more repetitive, and we began to settle in.

Settling In

My parents arrived on the group after the ballot for the blocks had been conducted. Having invested no energy in the development of the block to which they were originally assigned, they were able to move easily from it to the camp block, which had been vacated by an earlier settler. Usually, there was a reluctance to change after a family had settled down on a particular block. So much of an individual's labour and effort went into his own property that he quickly developed a close attachment to it. Apart from a few kilometres' distance from the town, there was very little difference in the quality of the various blocks. Some considered there was an advantage in having a riverside block, but for others this was offset by the danger of flooding.

Although we missed the ballot for the blocks, we were there in time for the ballot for the horses. This was an exciting event, partly because of the novelty, and partly because everyone was anxious to see which horse would be theirs. Each horse was numbered and the numbers put into a hat, while names of settlers were put into another hat; by the drawing of lots from both hats, it was decided which horse would be allotted to which person. The horses were good working animals, generally of similar age and in prime condition. Occasionally, a particular horse took a settler's fancy and there was an exchange by mutual agreement to accommodate this, but there was little to choose between the horses and there were no complaints about the outcome of the ballot. My father drew a nondescript brown Clydesdale that was received enthusiastically by the whole family and given the name of Bobby. He served us well for a few months, until he developed a tumour and had to be put down. He was replaced by another Clydesdale named Jack, and when we finally left the group it was everyone's hope that this hard-working, docile creature would find a good owner in our successor.

Although they were now proud horse owners, the settlers were not, by any stretch of the imagination, horsemen. They had no riding or handling skills. In the words of one of the few who did have some experience in this area, 'They didn't know which end kicked'. The varying temperaments of the animals were a mystery to the settlers, and the horses, sensing this vulnerability, trampled on toes and

The author leading Margery and Mary on the farm horse, 1927, with buildings of the adjacent farm in the background.

Scene taken from the same vantage point in 1993.

nipped their owners. A horse would often be led to a nearby stump so that the owner could mount from that advantageous position, rather than use the stirrup and risk displacing an insecurely fastened saddle. On one occasion, my father's attempt to assist an inexperienced rider to mount had Charlie Chaplin–like overtones. The man was short in stature and could not use the stirrup, so my father cupped his hands to form a step and heaved, intending to help him up into the saddle. But the effort was greater than required. To my father's surprise, instead of his friend finishing up in the saddle, he appeared on the ground on the opposite side of the horse. Fortunately, no injury resulted, and the humour of the situation outweighed the humiliation.

The quality of the cows that were made available to the settlers was not as good as that of the horses. They were a mixed lot. Those purchasing agents who did their job conscientiously sent some good cattle, but among the beasts supplied were a good number to which the historian G.M. Trevelyan's description of cattle on the commons in England in the eighteenth century could be aptly applied: 'starved, todbellied runts, neither fit for the dairy or the yoke'.* One might add that some were unfit for the butcher, having been bruised from rough handling on the journey down. The fear in their usually placid eyes betrayed the effects of the long journey they had undergone. They had been transported from the country by train to eastern ports, by ship across the Great Australian Bight, and then by train to the groups from the port. As a result, many were bewildered, frightened and wild from panic. They were driven on foot the 20 or 25 kilometres from the Margaret River railhead to the blocks, and consequently were not in the best of condition or temper on arrival. Each settler was allocated two or three cows to start with, to act as house cows. The herd was gradually built up as new animals came and as the early arrivals calved.

One of our cows was so wild on arrival that just as she reached the gate, she sped off into the bush, forded the river and ran wild

---

* G.M. Trevelyan, *English Social History*, 3rd impression, London: Longmans Green & Co., 1945, p. 300.

Mary and Margery with Dinky, the first calf born on the property. Note the land in the background, which was considered 'cleared'.

for some days, eluding every attempt to catch her. She was finally found and rounded in when we took a small herd of other animals through the bush, with a very docile one led behind a cart as a decoy. The wild cow joined the group, very gingerly at first but with increasing confidence, and by careful shepherding was led into the holding paddock. This animal must have experienced some very rough handling during transport, because she remained shy of human contact for a long time. When the time came for her to give birth to her first calf, we foresaw that milking would be difficult and so we constructed a race and a pen to contain her. The newly born calf was led up the race, with the mother following, until both were secured in the pen. The calf was left with the mother for a day or two instead of being separated at birth, as was usually the case. When the calf was finally removed, the cow was so terrified at the approach of humans that she thrashed around wildly and had to be secured by ropes on the horns and each leg so that she could be milked, and to prevent her harming herself. A loose rope was frequently used on the rear leg of a cow that was fractious or had a habit of kicking, but this was the only time we had to truss up an animal securely to be able to manage it. It was some weeks before the cow could be released to join the herd, and for the whole of the first lactation period she had to be driven up the race and secured in the pen before she could be milked. The restraining ropes were gradually removed as the animal became more docile. My father handled her gently and patiently and was rewarded at her second calving with a thoroughly domesticated mother manageable in the normal way. She was a beautifully marked cow, with black and white patches — we called her Beauty — and was one of the most prolific milkers in the herd.

All cows were given names. There were a Betty and a Molly among the early arrivals, and as the herd built up the search for names became a family pastime. With few exceptions, the cows answered to their own names. They responded as a herd to the call of 'Cup, Cup, Cup' at milking time, and when assembled for milking they would wait patiently until their name was called to come to the milking point. They even appeared to have a pecking order, and if one jumped the queue, or if a name was called in the wrong order, confusion reigned. The cows were allotted, in theory, to us children. This, in addition to being an encouragement to share in the chores of milking and the feeding of calves, gave us a proprietary interest in the welfare of the animals. We were fast learning how to be farmers.

As with all farms, there was the occasional dramatic and some-times traumatic incident that intruded upon the normal course of events, providing both a diversion and a topic for local conversation. Three such events were associated with the herd.

The first was when a cow named Ruby, an inveterate escaper from the paddocks, wandered to the edge of the river and slipped in. We found her mid-morning, swimming in the river, attempting unsuc-cessfully to gain a foothold on the steep banks. How long she had been in the water we did not know, because, as she was not a milker, she had not been missed at milking time. The river was quite deep at that particular stretch, and someone was despatched to a place where the opposite bank could be reached, so that the cow would not land on the far side and become lost in the thick bush that was there at the time. Word soon got round and neighbours gathered to watch and participate in the little drama. Ruby was cajoled by shouts and calls, enticed with food, and coerced more forcibly by sticks and stones thrown into the water from the far bank to frighten her out of the water. But all to no avail. Spot, our fox terrier, stimulated by the excitement of the occasion, joined in the fun and swam aimlessly around the animal, adding to her confusion. The gathering spectators proffered advice. Even lassoing was tried when the animal swam close to the bank. But it was no use. A slipway was dug to make a more gradual incline for the cow to exit the water, and a supply of hay was placed at the top of the slope, to act as an inducement. Finally, as night fell, the beast was left literally to sink or swim, as nothing more could be done until daylight. Sure enough, next morning, Ruby was standing quietly on the river bank at a safe distance from the water, having consumed all the fodder that had been left for her. Alas, poor Ruby never did her duty by producing offspring, and in so demonstrating her unsuitability for inclusion in a dairy herd ended up being disposed of to the local butcher.

Another mild drama was occasioned by one of the cows becoming bogged in the swampy creek bed. We heard her long, frantic lowing and found her up to her belly in mud, unable to get any leverage with her legs. She was quite unable to extricate herself and in danger of sinking further as she struggled in the soft ooze. Someone was posted to calm her down and to keep her head above water. Slings, improvised from ropes and sacking, were passed underneath her forequarters by means of forked poles pressed into the mud at an angle and fished for at the other side of her body. The slings were pulled into position underneath her and wrapped around her body in the form of a belt, just behind her forelegs. A rope was attached and thrown over the branch of a nearby tree, to divert the direction of the pull so that the slings would raise her upwards. With a few energetic but gentle heaves, the weight of the beast in the mud was eased, and slowly, reluctantly, the squelching mud yielded up its victim, none the worse for her experience.

On another occasion, Betty, a most docile Jersey cow, a favourite of the family and our best milker and cream producer, gave birth to twin calves and was unable to stand after the birth. We found her in a secluded dell in the bush, struggling but too weak to rise on her back legs. She lay there for a month, and just as arrangements were being made to put her down she regained her feet. During that month, she had to be fed and watered where she lay, which involved a trek of about half a kilometre. She also had to be milked, her milk being wasted on to the ground—a considerable loss to the meagre income of the farm at that time. The twin calves were both healthy and a welcome addition to the herd. Fortunately, Betty appeared to recover completely and produced several fine calves and much milk after that episode.

Breeding pigs were obtained at a later date and, of course, poultry was always kept, despite the ravages of foxes, goannas and dingoes. With no background in farming, we had to learn the day-to-day management of the farm as we went along. I say 'we' deliberately, because in our own way we children were learning simultaneously with our father. Sources of information were diverse. Theory was picked up from texts on dairying that my father had brought out from England, although much of their content was quite impractical and inapplicable to Australian conditions. From time to time, useful articles were published in the *Western Mail*, a weekly publication, and in various magazines that were handed round from settler to settler. There was much discussion whenever the settlers gathered together at social events, or during lunch breaks when they were working together on a project. A few people on the group had farming experience, and information and advice were offered freely. Much knowledge was transmitted in this way, but the most prolific source was the foreman, who was a mine of information on the practicalities of farming. He had a rough knowledge of herd management and was himself given guidance by a supervisor.

Life on a dairying property is one of the most consistently demanding of any form of farming venture. Milking has to be done twice every day, morning and night, at close to twelve-hour intervals. This results in a very long day. The whole family cannot leave the property together for even twenty-four hours without jeopardizing milk production. After each milking, the milk has to be separated to extract the cream, and the utensils and separating machinery thoroughly washed. Pigs, poultry and young calves have to be fed, and sick beasts and emergencies attended to. We had a small Lister separator that was turned by a manually operated handle and was very heavy to get started. To perform its task properly, it had to be kept going at a certain number of revolutions per minute, and a bell would ring if the operator slackened, letting the number of revolutions fall below the critical limit. It could be set to produce thick or thin cream. If the cream was too thin, it was downgraded by the butter factory and a dockage imposed. It was important, therefore, to ensure that the cream was thick enough to pass this test but not so thick as to reduce the maximum quantity that could be extracted from the milk.

The advent of a calf was always a welcome event, not only because it brought a new beast into the herd—a female calf was always hoped for in the early days—but also for its own sake. Calves were separated from their mother as soon as possible but were fed on their mother's milk for the first three days. They then received separated milk until they were able to take to the grass. After being parted from its mother, a calf would have to be coaxed to drink. We would encourage it to suck our fingers and then pour milk into the palm of the hand, letting the milk run along the fingers into the calf's mouth. As the calf became accustomed to this process, the level of the hand was gradually lowered until the calf's head dipped into a bucket containing milk. Over the course of a few days, the fingers were gradually submerged in the milk and then surreptitiously removed altogether. By this time, the calf, without being aware of it, was drinking from the bucket. The progression from one stage to another required considerable patience and could not be hurried. Anyone who has watched a calf feed will have seen it butting its mother hard with its head if it is not getting enough milk to satisfy itself. This also happened when it was being fed by hand, and care had to be taken to keep up the flow of milk, without waste. Later, one had to be sure that the feeding bucket was held firmly. Failure to do so would result in a calf with a bucket over its head, thrashing wildly about and bumping into everything in its path until it was released.

And so, gradually, we became absorbed in the continuous daily and seasonal aspects of farm life—always busy, full of activity, relieved of the necessity of detailed planning by the force of habit and the pressure of routine activities.

Everyday Life

EVERYDAY LIFE ON THE FARM was repetitious but never boring. Milking, clearing, fencing, draining and animal husbandry were continuous, but the seasons brought their special tasks and there were frequent interruptions to break the monotony of life.

Late spring was haymaking time. Except for some light grazing to encourage strong growth, cattle were barred from certain paddocks that were reserved for hay to supplement the sparse summer feed. The hay paddocks consisted of clover or oats, both of which grew luxuriantly. A prerequisite to mowing was the marking of hidden tree stumps, to avoid damage to the mower. Pieces of white rag were tied to long sticks, these home-made flags marking the presence of stumps invisible below the growing crop. The mown hay was allowed to lie where it fell and was turned with a hayfork two or three times. The hayfork was also useful for warding off aggressive magpies, which were breeding at this time of the year and would swoop down on the uncovered head of anyone who intruded into their territory.

Haymaking was a pleasant though tiring task, and the memory of the distinctive sweet aroma of the maturing hay can still be revived occasionally during a visit to the countryside in late springtime. When thoroughly dry, the hay was gathered into windrows with the mechanical hayrake and then stooked with the fork. As hay is not a heavy commodity, the spring cart was fitted out with frames at front and rear to maximize the load carried on each trip. One person would throw the hay into the cart using a long hayfork, while another person on top of the load would spread it out evenly for carting to the haystack. Harvesting is always a most anxious time, as rain on the hay as it lies drying in the field causes it to go mouldy and completely destroys its value as feed. One year, in his anxiety to avoid this happening to a particularly good crop that was badly needed for summer feed, my father made arrangements for five or six timber workers from the local timber mill to help gather in the crop in exchange for a home-cooked meal and a nominal payment of cash.

They were a cheerful group of men, their muscles strengthened by the hard work in the forest and at the mill. Despite the language barrier (for they were not long out from Europe), they not only worked well to gather in the crop in one day but they also seemed to enjoy it. My mother worked as hard as any to feed them with pork, freshly killed for the occasion, vegetables and dessert. She supplied them with morning and afternoon teas, sandwiches and home-made cakes, plenty of liquid in the field and a glass or two of beer or wine at the end of the day. I recall their boisterous cheerfulness as they gathered at the meal table at lunchtime, and wondered at their strange incomprehensible conversation — my first encounter with foreigners en masse. On reflection, they had good cause to be cheerful. The work was child's play compared to the heavy work of timber-cutting, and as they were living in single quarters, their wives and sweethearts still in Europe, the sumptuous home-cooked meal and family atmosphere must have provided a welcome contrast to their usual lonely bachelor meals of fatty, pan-fried meat and vegetables.

The Department of Agriculture was always willing to give settlers advice about experimental and opportunity crops. Field peas were grown one year and maize was a regular crop. What I remember most about these two crops is that the young peas provided a welcome variation to the vegetable menu for a few days while they were still tender, and the maize cobs provided the raw material for popcorn. One year, when potatoes were scarce and attracted high prices, the group foreman advised my father to plant a crop. It was a good one, with large, disease-free tubers. However, as many settlers in the South West had made a similar decision, the potato

market was flooded and prices plummeted. Thanks to the generosity of Mr Samworth, the Margaret River storekeeper, my father was lucky to exit the venture recouping the cost of seed and fertilizer. Again, the household table reaped some benefit and for several weeks we had a surfeit of potatoes: boiled, fried, battered and roasted. In all the variations of cooking this versatile vegetable, there is nothing to equal a small new potato boiled, or a well-matured large one roasted in its jacket and topped off with fresh farm butter.

On another occasion, there was a market in South Africa for clover seed and it was decided to reserve a section of a paddock for the purpose of seed gathering. A heavily flowering patch was chosen and allowed to go to seed. Some settlers gathered the burrs by means of sheep skins fitted to a roller, but in the absence of this contraption we had to be content with a more primitive and labour-intensive method. When the clover was thoroughly dry, a sieve was set up in the field. It consisted of a wire spring mattress of a type common at the time, having small holes about 0.5–0.75 centimetre in diameter. The mattress was set up at an angle by supporting props, the face pointing towards the direction from which the breeze

The author's sister Mary, with a pumpkin that grew wild on the property. The family was unfamiliar with this vegetable and had no idea of how to cook it. Note the closeness of the bush to the group cottage.

was blowing. The whole family was put to work raking up burrs, which were mixed with the dead stalks of the clover plants and sand. The material so gathered was shovelled to the top of the sloping sieve and as it fell through the holes in the mattress it was winnowed by the breeze. The sand, being heavy, fell close to the sieve, the burr fell next, and the lighter chaff and stalks were blown some distance away. This process was repeated several times, the product gradually becoming cleaner until an almost 100 per cent pure burr was collected and bagged for sale. It was hot, dusty and thirsty work in the scorching sun, but the experience links one in a very real way to the peoples of India and Asia, when one sees them threshing and winnowing their grain crops by centuries-old methods.

Eggs were collected twice daily, the fowls fed and watered and locked up at night to protect them from predators. The main predators were bobtailed goannas, which would steal the eggs. There were also foxes and dingoes, which plundered the fowlpens where the birds roosted at night. Spot usually coped with the goanna intruders very well. Avoiding the creature's bite, he would sink his teeth into a goanna's tail, swinging it round until it was stunned or managed to escape under a fallen log. Occasionally, when living close to nature, one has a rare demonstration of the sagacity of these canine friends. One such experience came to us when the dog, after disposing of a goanna that had taken a young chicken, carried the unharmed chick carefully in his mouth and deposited it alive at our feet. The wild thrashing of his tail as he was patted and fussed over revealed a near human delight in the outcome.

Foxes and dingoes were usually scared off by Spot's barking, but there was one particularly cunning animal that slipped through his guard and carried off a bird on several successive nights. My father naturally tired of this, so, not having a gun, he decided to lay a trap for the intruder. He baited a large fishhook with meat and secured it near the fowlpen. The next night, the animal took the bait and disappeared into the night, never to return. Whether it died or not we never knew, but my father asserted that this novel method at least gave the predator a sore throat. Incidents like this, trivial as they may seem, provided a topic of conversation and brought a bit of life to the isolated family.

Goats are notorious scavengers but cows usually adhere closely to their diet of pasture or hay. However, we had a cow that took a fancy to a treasured Fair Isle pullover belonging to my father. He had hung it on a post while he was working, and by the time it was rescued the sleeves had been demolished. Fortunately, the body of the garment was unharmed and, with the expertise of my mother, it was turned into a vest.

For us children, the daily routine was to round up the cows each morning, milk, separate the cream, feed the separated milk to the calves, and do one or two other jobs depending on available time. We always left home in time to walk directly and speedily to school (once it was established), 3 kilometres away. After school, there was the return walk home, and a repetition of the morning's chores before the evening meal. The weekends were taken up partly with various duties on the farm and partly in relaxation and playtime activities. My parents had a strong Protestant background, and apart from essential farm duties no development or general work was

The author's family, c. 1931. Note the cream separating shed in the background.

done on Sunday. This was mainly when we children went on our explorations and swimming expeditions.

There was, of course, no electricity. In the evenings, our after-dark activities were conducted by the light of a kerosene table lamp, the flame of which was fed by a cotton wick, or, if we wanted to be alone, by the light of a hurricane lantern. There were few late nights. We were usually tired after the activities of the day, but in the early evening we were occupied by the small amount of homework we had to do, reading, the assembly of our two precious jigsaw puzzles, or card games. Occasionally, with encouragement from my mother, we wrote a letter to our cousins in England. We also carried out a few evening chores, most of them related to the necessity for stretching the meagre family budget.

My mother always ensured that my father had a reasonable supply of tobacco, the one luxury allowed, as he derived considerable comfort from his short evening smoking session. To minimize cost, Havelock plug tobacco was cut into flakes with a sharp tobacco knife and rolled between the palms of the hands, before being put into his tobacco pouch. Cigarettes were made in a tiny cigarette machine consisting of a wide rubber band fixed at either end to two rollers. The rollers were separated, and Rizla brand cigarette paper was inserted and spread with tobacco—not too thickly, to make the supply stretch as far as possible. The rollers were closed and the cigarette rolled, the gummed edge of the paper then being licked and stuck down. To conserve matches, spills were made by tightly rolling strips of paper. These could be ignited from the kitchen fire and used to light the lamps or my father's pipe or cigarettes. Another evening task was the production of toilet paper: cutting any available newspaper into squares.

Maximum use was made of the milk and eggs available, and my mother produced delicious rice puddings, custards and bread-and-butter puddings. She made scones (which she always pronounced to rhyme with 'tones') and rock cakes and baked her own bread. Yeast was kept in bottles in the kitchen. Until my mother learned to control this volatile brew, there was an occasional explosion of a bottle or a loud 'Pop!' as a cork was forcibly expelled and the ceiling sprayed with the escaping yeast.

Because of shared activities, life on a farm brings a family close together. It also brings them closer to the totality of life's experiences than life in a city does, where activities are more specialized and separated. Procreation, birth, sickness, death and all the inevitabilities of mortal existence are experienced vicariously through the animal kingdom, even if they are not minutely analysed or speculated upon philosophically. The association of a roast joint or chicken with the necessity of killing a living creature is more immediate on a farm than it is when the sentient, vital animal is distanced from the consumer by the intervention of the abattoir, the butcher's shop or the fast-food outlet. And the various stages of the transition from milk to butter—the milking of cows, the separation of the cream, its maturing or souring, the stirring and gradual thickening of the cream until the buttermilk appears, and the washing, salting and final patting of the rich, yellow butter into shapes—are not even thought about by children who find their butter in the family fridge or displayed in labelled wrappers on the supermarket shelves.

(My childhood experience of butter-making proved useful later, when I was in the army. A farmer on whose property we were stationed at Dandaragan, near Moora, sold the troops large jars of cream. It soon went sour in the hot sun. As butter was in short supply, I gathered up what was, to the others, now useless cream and, much to the astonishment of the city-dwellers in the group, turned it into butter. The occupants of my tent enjoyed a good supply of butter for a few days, until the secret spread and supplies of sour cream dried up.)

The killing of a chicken was a frequent occurrence limited only by the need to sustain a viable number of breeders and layers. And what chickens they were! Seldom killed under seventeen weeks, they were plump and heavy with succulent breast meat: none of the scrawny eight to ten week old birds that are retailed today. Their range feed was supplemented by a small quantity of pollard mixed into a warm mash with household peelings and scraps, and occasionally a handful of wheat. No attention was paid to food conversion rates or balanced diets, and there was surprisingly little disease.

The slaughter of a cow or bullock was a much rarer occurrence, and we only had to put down one horse because of sickness. If an animal died or had to be shot because of sickness, the carcass was burned. Other killings were to cull unproductive cows from the herd, or of bull calves raised specifically for meat. There was no local abattoir; the butcher came and shot the animal on the farm, where it was skinned and quartered for removal. The family was provided with a small quantity of meat as part of the deal and permitted to dissect the suet for rendering down for dripping. Tripe, a delicacy appreciated only by my father, was not a valued portion of the carcass and was handed to us for cleaning and cooking. These activities were carried out in a matter-of-fact manner, except occasionally when a favourite cow or calf had to be slaughtered. At these times, there would be tears and the affected person usually took no part in the proceedings.

Despite the fantasies evoked by the film *Babe*, pigs are animals with which most people find it difficult to develop the kind of affectionate relationship that one often does with a cow or a horse. For this reason, on the infrequent occasions on which a pig was killed — usually Easter or Christmas — no one felt upset. There was a need for haste, so the whole family was called on to assist. My father would select the victim and at feeding time the unsuspecting creature would be rendered unconscious by a blow to the head. Its throat was cut and the carcass hung to bleed. In the meantime, my mother would prepare huge quantities of boiling water in which the pig would be immersed, in preparation for the removal of the hair. All the children, right down to the youngest — probably because she objected to being left out — participated in this, as the bristle had to be removed quickly after immersion. The most effective instrument for doing this was a tobacco-tin lid. The blunt edge of the tin could be used for scraping firmly, without cutting the skin of the pig or buckling under the considerable pressure needed to remove the hairs. The pig would then be cleaned and the carcass cut up.

In the absence of refrigeration, my father would distribute portions of the meat to neighbours, who had been warned in advance of the proposed kill. We, in turn, participated when an animal was slaughtered on a neighbouring farm. My mother cooked a roast to perfection, with the crackling crisp and crunchy. She would also cook English type pork pies — a delicacy eagerly anticipated. In her younger days, she worked at the home of an English Midlands family who conducted a chain of pork pie shops. Firkin's pork pies are still renowned in the West Bromwich district, although the original family died out some years ago. My mother had the recipe, which she guarded jealously. I recall her cutting up the meat into small pieces — no mince for her. Pastry was made from lard rendered from a pig killed at some earlier time, and the bottom and sides of the pie were moulded round a bottle. The prepared meat, slightly salted, was incorporated into the mould. Jelly made by boiling the pig's trotters was poured over the meat, then the top pastry put into position and crimped. The manufacture of these pies demanded a great deal of effort, typical of the tasks undertaken by women of that time. With no refrigeration, such work had to be done as the opportunity arose, when the raw materials became available. It put extra pressure on the housewife, but the results of my mother's exertions produced in the wood-fired Metters No. 2 stove were gastronomic delights that cannot be emulated by the packaged, microwaveable foods so temptingly displayed in today's supermarkets.

One year, we raised a turkey — an episode that became a minor saga. Someone had given my father a turkey poult, and the bird was bred for Christmas. It was a fine gobbler, with striking plumage and a magnificent bright red comb. It had the full range of the farm but usually hovered near the house, pecking at the plentiful supply of grass throughout the spring and enjoying its daily feed of pollard mash and wheat in the evening. As a rule, it was most approachable at feeding time, and we intended to kill it on Christmas Eve and prepare it for cooking the following day. However, as the fateful hour neared, the bird seemed to sense that something was afoot. When approached, it ran off into the bush, evading all attempts to capture it. We had no turkey that Christmas and had to content ourselves with the usual chicken substitute. The turkey enjoyed, or perhaps endured, its precarious freedom for another week. Exercising all the hunting skills I thought I had acquired from my reading of James Fenimore Cooper, I stalked it barefoot to avoid any sound and crept up on it downwind to avoid any scent. I deployed my sisters and friends to cut off any way of escape. I waited patiently behind bushes or fallen logs for long periods, hoping for its unsuspecting approach, but somehow at the last minute it always became aware of my presence and fluttered off out of harm's way. We finally triumphed on New Year's Eve, with the aid of a throwing stick, and it provided the main course for dinner on New Year's Day.

Even as our life was settling down into a regular pattern, clouds were forming on the horizon: the government's growing disinterest in the scheme, the falling price of butterfat, and the disheartening burden of interest payments. But these were problems for the future, and we were determined to make the best of the present.

Chapter Six

BUILDING A
COMMUNITY

LIFE WAS NOT ALL WORK AND DRUDGERY. Pleasure was sought, and obtained, from social activities of various kinds. The originators of the Group Settlement Scheme had recognized that social contact was an essential feature of group settlement: necessary not only as relief from the isolation of life on farms often out of sight of their closest neighbours, but also for the exchange of the chit-chat that characterizes any established community.

Social activities were nearly all self-generated. Radio had only recently been introduced to the cities and was certainly not accessible to this remote district. Of course there was no television (can the reader conceive of a world without it?). Until the school was built in 1929, social activities were held in a building (if indeed it could be described as a building) about 4 kilometres from our home. Situated on a fork in the road beyond where the Osmington Anglican Church and the monument to early pioneers now stand, it was a crude bush shelter supported by forked posts cut from straight saplings. The truss beams for the flat roof rested in the forks of these posts, the roof itself consisting of corrugated-iron sheets held in place by poles and heavy logs. In summer, fresh green bushes were usually placed on the roof to moderate the effect of the sun's rays. There were no nails used in the construction, as it was intended that the iron be reused once the temporary shelter was dismantled. Three walls were made of brushwood and ti-tree, something like the brushwood fences now seen in the suburbs of Perth, though not so neatly finished. The fourth side, the front, was left completely open.

Later, social and religious functions were transferred to the school. Various activities were held in this small but cosy building,

Group children at the 1927 Christmas party. Note the 'community centre' at the rear — a crude bush shelter with bushes on the tin roof to reduce the heat. This was the centre for all community activity, before the construction of the school. (Courtesy Mrs E. Carruthers)

usually once a month. There were whist drives, dances and, on special occasions such as Christmas, a general social evening with games, songs, and items rendered by those in the community who had a talent in a particular direction — and a few who did not but failed to recognize the fact. My father had brought out from England an assortment of exotic headgear, including bowler and Panama hats, a straw boater and an English peaked cap. He also had a cork-lined topee purchased in Ceylon on the way out. Once a year, these were lent to some of the more imaginative settlers, providing the means of enlivening the annual fancy-dress party. My mother and father were not unimaginative themselves on these occasions, frequently winning one of the modest prizes awarded. My mother used to sew late into the night to fit us and neighbouring children with costumes. One year, my father won a prize for his entry 'Sleepless Nights': he paraded in his pyjamas holding the latest born child of a neighbour's on one arm and my sister's doll on the other.

A special function held soon after the school opened in 1929 was a full-day picnic to celebrate the centenary of the State. The picnic centred round the children. There were organized games and races, with prizes provided for both winners and losers. Each child was given a bag of lollies and a small gift; I remember the boys received a bag of marbles. Those of school age also received the special

medal that was struck to commemorate the event and presented by the government of the day to all schoolchildren.

My mother was a good whist player and an enthusiastic dancer. During the early years, when her health was good, she would thoroughly enjoy these regular monthly outings. Milking would be put forward an hour or so on the appointed night, the horse would be harnessed up to the spring cart, and off the family would go in style. Once there, the horse would be tied to a post or a tree, waiting patiently until the function was over around 11.00 p.m. The first arrivals would arrange the school desks around the walls of the building. Sawdust supplied in generous quantities by the timber mill employees, together with wax scraped off a few candles, would be scattered on the floor. The children were then allowed to enjoy themselves, boisterously dragging heavy bags filled with sawdust around the floor until the surface shone like that of a classic ballroom. Among the dances of the time were the waltz, foxtrot, veleta, Pride of Erin, Gay Gordons and barn-dance. This last was always a favourite with us children, as it customarily involved the exchange of partners and we got to dance with an adult. The sets

were always popular—the eightsome reel, the lancers and the charleston. A children's set was usually arranged during these dances, we children, watching the movements of the adults, dancing with bedraggled enthusiasm a step or two behind the music. If one of the adults' sets was short of a participant or two, the oldest and most accomplished of the children were included to make up the set, a situation always awaited eagerly by those most likely to be chosen.

The older children sat in positions usually forbidden—on top of the desks, feet planted firmly on the seat—while the adults squeezed uncomfortably on to the narrow seats. As the younger children wilted, exhausted by the excitement, they would be comfortably and safely settled on the floor beneath the desks.

My father, who did not dance, was the 'tea boy'. At the appropriate time, he would have kerosene tins containing freshly

Then...

The Burton and Clark children dressed for a fancy-dress party, c. 1929. Left to right: The author, Edna Clark, Moira Clark, Mary Burton, Margery Burton

...and now

The same group, in 1994.
Left to right: The author, Mary Burton, Moira Rodgers, Edna Carruthers, Margery Morley

brewed tea and coffee ready to go with the supper. Supper was usually provided by the women bringing a plate of food, but on special occasions sandwiches and cakes were purchased from a caterer in Margaret River. My father was seldom alone: there were a number of non-dancers among the men who would come to chat with him, and occasionally one of the dancers would come outside to steal a draw on a cigarette and to 'sit this one out'. In any case, my father was content with his own company, and the sight of him sitting on a log before a blazing fire, the fiery glow of the flames playing on his face as he puffed contentedly at his pipe, would have made a subject worthy of any artist.

The Anglican rector at Margaret River, Rev. Edward C. Dawson, was an enthusiastic and effective scoutmaster in the Baden-Powell tradition. His wife, Irene, conducted the guides, and their trusted companion and help, Salvationist Rose Bishop, who travelled with them wherever they went, supervised the cubs. On one Friday evening in each month, Rev. Dawson would drive the parish utility in all directions, collecting the members of the troop from outlying locations. I would set off as soon as possible after school, overnight gear in a kitbag, and walk 2 or 3 kilometres so that he would not have to travel the full distance to the farm. The scout meetings were held in the church hall at Margaret River and after the parade the whole troop slept in the hall or in tents set up in the church grounds. Scouting activities continued on Saturday morning, until we were returned home by utility about midday.

There were many highlights of my scouting days. In summer, we occasionally went swimming in the nude at the mouth of the Margaret River, which in those days was inaccessible to motor vehicles. The parish utility was parked at the end of the road and we made our way past a derelict house, through the scrub, and over the sandhills to the isolated swimming spot. Another highlight was a fortnight's camp at Quindalup, then a desolate strip of coastal scrub

State Centenary Picnic, 1929: line-up for the women's sack race on the road outside the school. Back row (left to right): K. Rawlings, Mrs A. Neale, Mrs Jones, author's mother, Mrs G. Gee Front row: Mrs Spry, Mrs A. Thorne, D. Piggot

near Busselton. Yet another was a concert put on by the senior boys, with some outside assistance, under the direction of the scoutmaster. This concert was taken on the rounds of the various communities in the district and had full houses on each occasion. As far as I can recall, this was the only entertainment put on by a party outside the group during the five and a half years we spent in the district.

There was an occasional silent movie shown at a hall in the town by an itinerant promoter. The only one I attended was *All Quiet on the Western Front*, the first of such picture shows, which received considerable publicity.

The annual agricultural show was a feature of most districts. We attended the first of the Margaret River district shows, which was held in a paddock on the hill to the left of the road just beyond the bridge at the northern edge of the town. We also attended the first show held in the new permanent showgrounds on the other side of the town, near the railway station. It was opened by the then Premier, James Mitchell (later Lieutenant Governor Sir James Mitchell), from the back of a truck.

Country shows, with their sweet and food stalls and sideshows, are held in more populous centres today but no doubt hold the same fascination for children as those earlier ones. In our family, there was no spare cash for entrance to sideshows or for extravagant spending on non-essentials, but we did not feel deprived. There was plenty of entertainment to be had from the numerous sideshow spruikers as they vied for the custom of patrons. There was the raucous promoter of the boxing troupe, trying to incite locals into taking on his champions of contests in other parts of the country. There was the owner of the high-striker, who would try to persuade his audience — for a fee — to strike the button on the base of the contraption with a heavy iron-headed mallet. Anyone who managed to hit it with enough force to ring the bell at the top would receive a prize. There was an oily gentleman who would guess your weight to within a pound by running his hands over your arms, body and legs. He would take the women on without any contact. There were a sword-swallower and a flame-eater. But the greatest attraction of all was the trapeze artist, who set up his taut rope in the open for a preview of the real show he would later put on behind a canvas screen. His sure-footed exploits with his soft shoes and long balancing pole drew gasps of admiration from the children in his audience as he negotiated the wire, occasionally faking a false step.

There were few deviations from routine, a notable exception being a picnic trip to Busselton, about 60 kilometres from the group. It was a momentous event in which most of the families of the district participated. A truck belonging to one of the settlers on the adjoining group and another truck hired from town were fitted out with rough seating down the middle. The adults sat back to back on the seats, older children crowded on as best they could, with the younger children being accommodated on laps. Possibly because she was slim, my mother was one of two women who squeezed alongside the driver in the front seat of the cab, with two of the smaller children on their laps. The excitement of the outing was a sufficient antidote to the discomfort of the transport.

The day was an adventure for us children, with its long ride into the unknown, its beach activities and the mile-long walk out on the timber jetty, which in those days was a hive of activity. We watched, fascinated, as a shunting engine pulled railway trucks laden with sleepers out to a waiting ship, returning with long rakes of empties to be distributed to the numerous timber mills in the surrounding forests, for refilling.

However, it turned out to be a disastrous day for my parents. In the first mishap, Spot was run over. Following his canine instincts for comfort, the frisky fox terrier, tired of the excitement, had sought shelter under the tray of the truck, just in front of the rear wheel, and had settled down for a rest. No one noticed him, and when the truck started off the rear wheel ran over Spot, seriously injuring his leg. There was some consternation among the adults, but the injury was apparently not serious enough to warrant putting the animal down. He was made comfortable in the shelter of a neighbour's house, supplied with water and left for the day. The excitement of the outing soon erased the event from our childish minds, but when we returned home that evening we found that Spot had dragged himself about a kilometre back to our own home and was waiting for us on the back verandah. There was a sad and soulful greeting for us all, with none of the customary tail wagging, as he was obviously in pain. There must have been considerable damage, because he languished for a few days, pampered by the whole family. He received no veterinary assistance, which would probably have prevented some of the disfigurement resulting from the injury. Over a few weeks, Spot gradually recovered. Although he had sustained permanent damage to the leg, his previous unbounded zest for life was undiluted. He continued in good health and high spirits during the rest of our stay on the group.

On arrival at Busselton, my parents did some shopping at one of the larger stores, where there was a bigger range of goods than at Margaret River. This was the beginning of their second misfortune. When they returned to the shop to collect their purchases of household linen and bedclothes, on which they had spent a sizeable sum, they found them stolen. The shopkeeper said that they had been collected earlier. The shop accepted no responsibility and my parents never recovered the parcel. Its loss was a great blow to them, as they had dug deeply into the cash reserves brought from England, which they had no hope of replenishing from their meagre income.

The trip home was a noisy one, as a number of the party had spent some of their time in the Busselton hotels. My mother, who hated the effects of alcohol, later vehemently expressed puritanical disgust at the boisterous but harmless conduct. Fortunately, she was insulated to a great extent by her position in the front cab. The heavy intake of liquids accelerated the call of nature, and periodically the truck driver was persuaded, by vigorous pounding on the roof of the cab, to stop at the next heavily wooded section of the road. There ensued a hasty flight from the vehicle by both the hard-pressed and the opportunists: the men to one side and the women to the other, as if directed by an invisible master of ceremonies.

Relieved and reassembled, the party continued with raucous jollity and hearty song until the next enforced stop or until sheer fatigue triumphed. One by one, they lapsed into subdued concentration, intent only on avoiding being dislodged from their seats as the truck swung round a bend or bounced over an unexpected pothole, and on protecting the children, most of whom had fallen into fitful and exhausted slumber on the tray of the truck.

Nurturing Minds
and Souls

EDUCATION IS ALWAYS A PROBLEM in isolated regions, and the fact that there was no school available when we first arrived on the group was of great concern to my parents. The community was without a school for over two years. It was a policy of the Education Department that a school would be built and a teacher provided in a district only if an average attendance of at least twelve children could be guaranteed over a three-month period. The group families had a number of children but many, including my youngest sister, Mary, were not yet of school age, and others were over fourteen, the school leaving age at the time. Children were required to assist on the property as soon as they turned fourteen, and few went on to secondary and higher education.

At first, we had to make do with correspondence lessons under the willing but, because of other duties, inadequate supervision of my busy mother. It was not until Bonola's timber mill moved into the district, with a few families with children of school age, that the requisite guarantees of sufficient attendance were accepted by the Education Department and the school building was erected. It opened on 16 April 1929 to the great relief of all the families of the district. The school was at first called the Airdale school, but that was inappropriate, as Airdale was the name given to Group 84 and the school was situated within the boundaries of Group 85. It was renamed Group 84-85 school in October. And so it remained officially, although it was always known locally as Group 85 school, until in 1935 the group was named Osmington after a village in Dorset with which one of the original families of the group had connections.

It was a one-teacher school, and the dedication of those early

Osmington school, being used as a polling place. (Courtesy Mrs E. Carruthers)

teachers and their influence on the lives of their pupils—and in many cases on the life of the community—are seldom recognized today. They were isolated from their families and peers and, by today's standards, primitively boarded, usually with a local childless family, to avoid any appearance of favouritism. They were provided with the bare minimum of aids and support. Theirs was a life of devotion and dedication, which was generally recognized and appreciated by the community in which they served. The weak and unsuited rapidly gave up, but those who persisted were leaders and organizers of community activities, respected by adults and regarded with mixed awe and affection by their pupils.

When the Group 85 school opened, the Education Department could not immediately supply a permanent teacher, so the wife of a settler on the adjoining Group 84 was engaged on a temporary basis.

Mrs Mansfield, a trained teacher, thus became the first teacher at the school. A few months later, Mrs Coombes was appointed as the first permanent departmental teacher. She had spent a considerable time in South Africa, and her descriptions of life in that country planted in me the first seeds of a desire to see something of the wider world, especially a wish to see the then little known and isolated Victoria Falls. I have been fortunate in having travelled widely in my adult years, but this particular dream was never to be fulfilled. Mrs Coombes was followed by Miss Pell, a slender, frail young woman who, because of ill health, only stayed a fortnight.

The next teacher was Mr W.J. Caskey, our first experience of a male teacher. He, too, had a relatively brief stay of only a few months, and left the school in May 1931. I have enduring memories of this teacher, as, before he left, he distributed many of his personal library books to the children of the school. I received a beautiful copy of the poems of Lord Byron, elegantly bound in soft leather. I read the poems avidly at the time and still treasure the book inscribed with his signature. This was the first 'adult' book I had received, and although I was too young to appreciate much of it then I have returned to it from time to time and am sure that it, and the circumstances of receiving it, influenced my thinking and subsequent choice of literature. Tragically, as we learned shortly after his departure, Mr Caskey was lost at sea in a yachting accident off Rottnest Island.

The next teacher, who was still at the school when we left the district in 1932, was Miss Cook, a very caring teacher much loved by children and parents alike.

Teaching in a one-teacher school must have been difficult and demanding, but somehow the system worked and we absorbed a great deal of basic learning. Some lessons involved the whole school, but when the lesson did not concern us we became adept at shutting out what was happening elsewhere and concentrating on our own exercises.

We had our various duties, such as lighting the fire in winter, cleaning the blackboards, filling inkwells and changing blotting paper, and looked forward to being selected for these little extra tasks. There were days of excitement when parcels would arrive from the Education Department and new texts, exercise books, pads and pencils were distributed. I remember the day when the first books for our 'library' arrived, purchased with funds provided by the Parents and Citizens Association. This support group ran dances, whist drives and other activities for the provision of 'extras' for the school. On this day, we were permitted to select a book to read and were given an extended reading time to allow the novelty to wear off. We were also allowed to re-enter the classroom early after lunch if we wished. My first selection was *Tom Brown's Schooldays*. Nature studies were supplemented, in a practical way, by the profusion of material in the surrounding bush. To reinforce one of our geography lessons, we kept accurate records of the movement of the earth round the sun by means of daily markings of the length of the shadow thrown at twelve noon by a particular post in the school grounds.

The personality of the teacher played a great part in the life of the community, and teaching in such a small community demanded diplomatic skills of the first order. The teacher was comforter in the event of accidents at school, consoler in times of distress, and on at least one occasion even health worker, examining the heads of all children during an outbreak of head lice.

It surely says something for the dedication and character of these early teachers that in later life at least three of the first intake of pupils in 1929 obtained Bachelor of Arts degrees through mature-age studies, two at The University of Western Australia and one at La Trobe.

The location of the school and the regular attendance of the pupils provided a further amenity unrelated to education but important in the lives of the settlers. The post office sent out a circular advising that in the future all mail for farms in the district would be delivered to, and could be collected from, the school site. Each family was required to erect a mailbox with their name on it, for the receipt of mail and newspapers. The boxes were a motley lot manufactured mostly from kerosene tins, pinewood kerosene cases and small drums, but they served their purpose. There was occasionally a more elaborate one produced with pride by someone with carpentry skills. They were erected on the appointed spot near the school, at the end of the made road, looking for all the world like a cluster of surreal toadstools. Twice a week, the children would bring any letters written by the family and leave them in the box. The mail contractor would collect these, leaving in return any incoming mail and, for those who ordered them, the newspapers. The weekly publication the *Western Mail* was the most popular newspaper of the period among country people, taken by most until the Depression hit hard and they were forced to cancel their subscription to this last regular contact with the outside world. After school, the children would clear the boxes and take the mail home to their parents, who in most cases were anxiously awaiting news from 'the old country'.

Just as they were concerned about the lack of schooling available on the group, my parents, especially my mother, were concerned that the religious needs of the settlers were not well catered for. Both of them were Congregationalists. They were, although theirs was too simple a faith to have recognized it, liberal in outlook and tolerant of people of other denominations and religions. However, they valued the influence of religion on their children's lives.

With only thirteen families in the group, plus a few from the neighbouring Group 84, there was quite a mixture of denominations among the settlers, as well as some people who had no religious affiliations at all. There were Catholic and Anglican priests in Margaret River and a Congregational centre in Busselton, with a further centre to be opened at Cowaramup within a few months. But all were too far away for settlers on Group 85 to attend church regularly. Naturally, with so few adherents, and with the population being so scattered, local services were irregular. Those services that were held had a social as well as religious significance, and most of the Anglicans and non-conformists in the group attended the services of both denominations, as did a sprinkling of other settlers from Group 84. This tended to assist both denominations in making up the numbers to warrant holding a service. Not that it was ever worthwhile in financial terms, the ministries of both denominations being supported by home mission grants from central bodies in Perth and often from further afield.

The first religious gathering we attended was a baptismal service arranged by Ralph Featherstone, a young Congregational trainee based in Busselton. Held at the primitive bush shelter described in Chapter 6, it was an episode that would have merited a place in Steele Rudd's *On Our Selection*, a book about life among outback settlers and one of the most popular Australian light novels of the time. The minister was to have ridden out on horseback from the nearby village of Cowaramup for the service, the first to be held in the district since our arrival some months before. Being regular churchgoers in England, my parents missed this aspect of life and it was natural that my father should decide to attend.

The distance to the meeting place was considered too great for my mother, with Mary to care for, so Margery and I accompanied him, both dressed in our 'Sunday best'. My father was immaculately dressed for church in English style — navy blue suit, starched collar, walking stick and bowler hat. Despite the coolish day, he was a little dishevelled after the hour-long walk there. His polished shoes were covered in dust and his collar not a little crumpled. We children were blissfully unaware of anything strange, but the arrival of this apparition among the other settlers, who were dressed mainly in dungarees and open-necked shirts, obviously raised eyebrows among the established groupies. My father, with his puckish sense of humour, carried off the occasion with great aplomb and it became the subject of much good-humoured banter in many a subsequent conversation. Needless to say, he never made the same mistake again, and the blue suit lay carefully stored in mothballs during most of our years in the bush.

For some reason I can't recall, on this occasion the preacher did not arrive and it was decided to sing a few hymns and take up a collection while waiting for him. Well-known hymns were chosen, the singing being led by a Scotsman, an outgoing person and natural leader prominent in all community activities. The first hymn went well and the offering was taken up on a 'collection plate' consisting of the lid of a shoebox brought as a container for someone's picnic lunch. The well-known 'Abide with Me' was being sung heartily when Simon, the dog belonging to the Scot who was leading the singing, slunk into the group and set himself up immediately in front of his master. Stimulated by the sombre music, he pointed his nose in the air and emitted a long drawn out, doleful howl. This was too much to be tolerated, and at the line 'Shine through the gloom and point me to the skies', a well-planted boot to the appropriate part of the dog's anatomy pointed him firmly in that direction. His master's action, executed with hymn book held high while still singing heartily, turned the howling into a sharp squeal of pain, and the astonished hound burst through the scrub wall of the hut in his haste to escape the possibility of a further assault. Triggered by a muffled giggle, the whole assembly burst into fits of uncontrollable laughter and the solemnity of the occasion was shattered.

The first religious service held in the new school was an Anglican service conducted by Brother Moore. Most of the settlers attended, irrespective of denomination, and although my parents did not attend we children were encouraged to go. I have a vivid memory of trudging along the unmade bush track with several other children. About a kilometre from the school, a decrepit T-model Ford chugged to a halt and the driver, a cassocked priest, called out, 'Are you going to the service?'. On the affirmative reply, the invitation to 'jump in' was extended and we crowded in on the vacant seats. That this unexpected ride was so firmly planted in my memory as a notable event has never ceased to surprise me. Such happenings, simple though they were, were rare in those times and in that place. It is a matter for interesting speculation, in these days of diversity and familiarity with the motor car, as to what kind of event will evoke such vivid memories in the minds of our grandchildren after sixty years. I recall also, probably with unfairness to Brother Moore, wondering whether we would have missed out on the ride if we had not been going to the service.

Brother Moore was followed by Rev. Dawson, who was known to me mainly through his activities as scoutmaster rather than as priest. I recall one special service in the Group 85 school when the Bishop of Bunbury confirmed several candidates from the district. During that same visit, although not an Anglican, I acted as god-parent to a fellow scout who was being christened prior to his confirmation. Rev. Dawson left Western Australia for England in 1931, to take up work in the parish of St John, in Clifton, Bristol. After a short period there, he was appointed Archdeacon of Mauritius, where he again became heavily involved in scouting activities. He died there from a heart attack, at the age of sixty-three, and his ashes were scattered at sea in accordance with his wishes. His widow became a field worker with the Mothers Union, a Church of England women's organization, and spent some years in the Republic of Honduras in that capacity.

The Rev. Reg Salter, minister of the Congregational churches at Cowaramup and Margaret River, was a tireless worker for the struggling settler and the underdog. He would come out for the Congregational service once a month, accompanied by his wife, who played the hymn tunes on a tiny portable harmonium. Rev. Salter was an enthusiastic preacher and we children would watch with fascination as the saliva gradually built up in the corners of his mouth when he warmed to his subject. The trials and difficulties of the settlers during the Depression weighed heavily on the heart and mind of this kindly man who sacrificed much, both of himself and his family, for the spiritual and material welfare of the people among whom he worked. He organized a supply of second-hand clothing and reading materials from his contacts in the city, and when he went fishing in Cowaramup Bay, many of his parishioners benefited from a good catch. He suffered severely from asthma, and his untimely death from the ravages of that exhausting complaint was hastened, I believe, by the neglect of his own welfare in the interests of others. His contribution to the community has been perpetuated in the naming of a street after him in Gracetown, on the lovely Cowaramup Bay.

On more than one occasion, Rev. Salter hammered together a makeshift coffin from pine cases for a settler's family who could not afford an undertaker to conduct a funeral. Even when they were held, funerals were not elaborate affairs. I remember my father's horror at the first he attended. After the church service, the coffin was placed on a utility vehicle, the mourners piling on also and sitting on the coffin for the ride out to the cemetery, which was some distance from the Margaret River township. Such was the pragmatism associated with life — and death — on the groups.

CHAPTER
EIGHT

NATURE

To those transported into it from a city environment, particularly from the heavily populated urban centres of the English Midlands, the dense, virgin bushland of the South West appeared a frightening and awesome place. In fact, it was not dangerous. There were no hostile inhabitants—no indigenous inhabitants at all by the time we arrived—and there were no dangerous animals. The creature to be feared most was the tiger snake, but even that reptile, except in October and November when it is drowsily emerging from its winter hibernation, seeks to avoid intruders and will slither away at the sound of approaching footsteps.

My mother was timid and never became completely comfortable with the bush and its isolation. She always had lurking fears of the children getting lost, falling into the river, being bitten by a snake or charged by a bull. My father's efforts in clearing and taming the bush overcame all sensitivity to it, and he had little time to relax and appreciate its subtly changing moods. Given more time, I'm sure he would have enjoyed the bush with childlike enthusiasm. Even so, he never failed to stop what he was doing if we children were around, to bring to our attention some aspect of nature newly discovered— an unusual flower, a rare green lizard angrily poking out its tongue, a racehorse goanna cornered up a tree, or a baby kangaroo abandoned by its mother during a chase with a dog. He never killed unnecessarily, always setting any captured specimen free, and forbade us to pick orchids or rare flowers or to hunt native animals.

To us children, the bush was paradise: mysterious, exciting, filled with unknown adventure but docile enough not to be feared. Any child who has not spent at least a few months in the country, preferably deep in the bush, unrestrained by the 'do's and don'ts' of city-bred parents, has missed out on the sense of oneness and dependence that comes only from close contact with nature. They have in a very real sense been deprived.

In those early days, less than a fifth of the land on the surveyed blocks had been even partially cleared. The rest, and the unsurveyed areas of departmental land, were in a condition close to virgin bush. The sleeper-cutters had gone through only a few years before, but the scrub had recovered so as to obliterate nearly all trace of their intrusion. A person could be within 3 or 4 metres of one of their fallen trees and not know it was there. The excitement of bursting through the thick undergrowth and finding oneself in the middle of a small clearing surrounded by huge chunks of wasted wood—the remains of some sleeper-cutter's exertions—was as great to us children as that felt by a prospector stumbling upon his golden nugget. We knew that our find would provide enough ready-cut firewood to fuel our fires for a month or more. After we rushed home to tell our father, the horse would be harnessed and we would wend our way back, to load up the wood and bring it home triumphantly. So profligate were those early hewers of sleepers that it would often take two trips to bring all of the spoils home.

The daytime atmosphere of the deep bush is one of peace and ambient stillness rather than silence. In summer, one hears the harsh 'Caw! Caw!' of the crows drawled out in lively crescendo and then gradually dying away in echoing cadence, as if the creatures from which the sound emanated had tired and fallen off to sleep. There is the conversational chatter of the magpies; the excited 'Twenty-eight! Twenty-eight!' of the parrots repeated over and over again; the sharp twittering of the smaller birds as they dash from bush to bush. As one moves through the undergrowth, one hears the swish of a startled bird as it escapes from its bush perch, or the soft rustle of short grass as a disturbed snake or lizard slithers out of harm's way. Occasionally, in the denser thickets, the 'Thump! Thump!' of a startled kangaroo or wallaby suddenly breaks the stillness.

In winter, the wildlife is less in evidence. Reptiles lie torpid underground in their winter sleep. Birds huddle in the dryness of a treetop hollow, or perch dolefully with feathers wrapped tightly round shivering bodies as they await the return of a sunny spell and warmth. But the forest is still enlivened by the heavy dripping of water from the leaves and bushes after a shower. So dense are the trees and shrubs in the untouched bush that hardly a drop of rain hits the ground before being intercepted by a tree or some undergrowth. The 'Drip! Drip! Drip!' continues long after a shower has stopped. At least, that was how things were when the area was being pioneered. Today one would probably have to search much farther off the beaten track to find the sounds of solitude that were commonplace then.

Nature's noises of the night have probably entirely gone by now; they were gradually disappearing during the years we were there. Then, as darkness fell, the activities of daytime creatures ceased and the daylight sounds fell silent. But as one stood under the brightly starlit sky, one was circumfused by the distinctive sounds of the night. All around, nearly always in the far distance, could be heard the subdued howling of dingoes. The barking of dogs disturbed by foxes or other intruders who ventured near their homesteads was clearly audible from farms kilometres away. In the early evening, as one moved deeper into the bush, there were the thudding of kangaroos and the softer padding of wallabies as they foraged for their evening meal. Sometimes, the glitter of an opossum's eyes could be seen in the low banksia or she-oak trees. In the later hours, one could occasionally hear, quite near at hand and clear above the ambient noises of the distance, the low monotone of the Australian owl as it went about its nocturnal activities: 'Mopoke! Mopoke!'

We children explored the thick ti-tree swamps that lined the creek beds, crawling on all fours along the tunnels made by quokkas as they criss-crossed the matted undergrowth. As far as possible, we avoided freshly made tracks indicated by recent droppings, preferring the older tracks, which were usually drier. These also had their inconveniences in the form of spider webs, from which hung brightly coloured, star-shaped spiders. They were apparently harmless, as we never suffered from spider bites. In any case, we always went armed with a stout stick to demolish any webs obstructing our path and to frighten off any snake, lizard or goanna that we might encounter. In fact, we seldom came across any of these creatures, although we often heard them scurrying ahead, our noisy passage through the undergrowth obviously frightening them away. We were further protected by the fact that we were usually accompanied by Spot, who scampered joyfully ahead, nosing the ground in excited chase of some invisible prey and incidentally clearing our path. If we had ever had a serious encounter, we probably would have retreated in haste and been dissuaded from further adventures.

We learned to navigate our way through the bush as if it were our native habitat, and never feared being lost no matter how dense the growth. Observation and memory play a great part in bush navigation, particularly if one intends to return by the same route. We kept our sights on the trees, looking for outstanding specimens, peculiar limb formations, the particular forms of dead branches, and anything of note in the fallen trees obstructing our path. We also frequently looked back so that we could recognize the path when we returned; the striking features of the bush often appear quite different when viewed in reverse. We were never lost nor felt insecure wherever we were in the bush. In any case, although the area we explored appeared quite vast to us as children, we were in no danger, as it was bounded on four sides by established tracks with which we were familiar and which were never more than about 2 kilometres apart.

Each change of season brought its familiar hallmarks, which we learned to anticipate as keenly as any primitive forest dweller. Late spring or early summer brought the reptiles out of their winter sleep. This was the time at which snakes were most dangerous, being still very sleepy, and we would have to exercise care to avoid coming on them suddenly. They were most likely to be found on an open patch of sand or in the ashes of a burnt out log, waiting for the rays of the sun to revitalize their torpid bodies. Summer brought its unremitting heat and cloudless skies. With the approach of autumn came humid March days, thunderstorms and, at night, the continual play of lightning all around, which could be glimpsed at certain vantage points through the ringbarked trees. As autumn faded, we were rewarded with field mushrooms appearing magically in the clover heavy with dew.

Winter brought its storms and high winds and the need to be more than usually alert to the danger of falling branches. As the season ended, the cold nights of September brought frosts that turned paddocks white. By the later years of our period on the group, we children had outgrown the Wellington boots we had brought out from England, and were reduced to one pair of shoes each. To prevent them from wearing out on the rough, often gravelly tracks, these shoes were reserved for special occasions, and, as was common among children of the time, we went about barefoot. Most of the time, this was no hardship, as the soles of our feet soon became as hard as leather. But passage over the crunching frozen clover was torture to our bare feet as we rounded up the cows on cold spring mornings. We looked forward to the warmth of the sun or the arrival of more wet weather, when it was not as cold. At the time, my sisters and I were puzzled that our mother always refused to allow us to be photographed in bare feet. We realized later that in England, a barefoot child indicated extreme poverty, and Mother did not want any inkling of our situation to be conveyed to relatives there.

Spring was glorious and eagerly awaited. There was always something blossoming in the bush, but spring was the season when the flowering plants came to life. The first of the true spring flowers was the purple hovea, in a number of varieties. The most spectacular of these was a raceme about 30–50 centimetres in height. Its single stem was surrounded by brilliant purple flowers in such profusion that it was completely hidden, the flowers appearing to stand unsupported, suspended in the surrounding scrub. As clearing of the bush progressed, this variety, or rather the more striking specimens of it, gradually disappeared until it became extremely

rare in the district. Kangaroo paws and wattle grew in profusion. Spider orchids were plentiful but grew singly and, being small, with their sombre colours blending in with their surroundings, had to be sought out. Donkey orchids and cowslip orchids grew in clumps and were chanced upon rather than sought. Like the hovea, all of these plants gradually became rarer, and even during the five years that we were on the group the more showy stands and specimens were encountered less frequently.

The various species were well known to us, even though we did not know their botanical names. We learned to distinguish between the 'blackboys' and the 'grassgins', both slow-growing trees of similar superficial appearance, with black trunks and grassy tops. The mature blackboys bore a spectacular spike covered in white flowers; when dry, these spikes made a stout walking staff. The trunks of dead blackboys, with their laminated, resin-impregnated layers, made ideal material for starting fires. The grassgins, or blackgins as they were sometimes called, had a softer, spongy trunk that was useless for burning. They bore a cluster of flowers that looked like drumsticks—each a longish handle with a knob at the end. When young, these two plants were less easy to differentiate, and we learned from painful experience that while the grassy tops of the blackboys were brittle and broke off easily, the grassgins were razor sharp and cut the fingers if one grabbed them by mistake when on the move.

We made whistles out of fresh gum leaves by removing all but the thin skin on one section of the leaf. When the young red tips were about to mature, we would seek out the largest ones and compete to see who could strip them of the layer of thin skin that covered them at this stage of their growth, without breaking it.

Water always holds a fascination for children, and the creek that ran through our block and the river that formed one of its boundaries were no exception. The uncleared creek basins were dotted with bushes of red flowering boronia standing out in vivid contrast against the thick mat of dark green ti-tree. If you were prepared to wade through the flooded banks in knee-deep water, you would find the dark brown and yellow scented variety that is sold on the streets of Perth in early spring. This is a smaller growing plant and we sought it eagerly because of its distinctive perfume. It was hard to find among the ti-tree, so instead of trying to spot it with our eyes we used to search for it by its scent, like fox hounds sniffing for their prey.

The waters of the creek held gilgies: small, almost transparent lobster-like creatures about the size of a prawn. Although they were edible, we used to catch them for fun, just as city children catch minnows, and then let them go unharmed. The river was home to the now famous marron: the freshwater lobster whose flesh is regarded by gourmets as a delicacy. They bred profusely in the pool just below our house. We would sit on a fallen log jutting out from the edge of the bank and dangle a piece of meat or bacon rind on a string — real-life Huckleberry Finns! When we felt the marron take the bait in its claws — and we never had to wait very long — we gently pulled the bait, with the prey attached, towards the surface of the water. A net attached to a long pole was already submerged in the water so as not to cause any ripples to disturb our quarry. As the bait with the marron clinging eagerly to it neared the surface, the net was slowly manoeuvred underneath the catch. When the marron became aware of the danger, it let go of the bait and, with a sudden frightened jerk, flipped backwards into the waiting net. Our family never developed a taste for this delicacy and we either released the marron directly into the river after capture or took them up the bank and let them edge their way, instinctively, backwards into the water. My own aversion to marron probably derived in part from the sense of horror I felt when I first saw them cooked and heard the sharp squeak of pain as they were dropped into boiling water.

The river was the venue for other pleasurable activities in summer—canoeing and swimming. The canoe belonging to children on the adjoining property had been made out of a single sheet of corrugated iron bent up to a point at one end to form the bow and fastened on to the square end of a kerosene case at the other to form the stern. The corrugations were flattened out as far as possible at these ends, with any residual apertures being caulked with rags. When not in use, the canoe was always kept in a thicket a little way removed from the swimming hole. A watch had to be mounted when we were canoeing, to alert us to the unwelcome approach of any adult across the adjacent open paddock. On the alarm being given, the canoe would be returned to cover in the thicket and we would resume our innocent swimming activities. This secrecy was not because of any prohibition on canoeing but because the sheet of iron, which was naturally a good one with no nail holes, had been obtained without permission. Retribution would no doubt be in store for anyone caught lifting such a valuable piece of property. We all took part in the exercise without any qualms of conscience and without asking too many questions. We younger ones were usually used as lookouts and were rewarded with an occasional ride in the canoe for this service and for not telling. I used to enjoy the thrill of these infrequent rides and was determined to build a canoe of my own when I got older. I had just been introduced to James Fenimore Cooper's *The Last of the Mohicans*,

and was at the stage of stalking through the bush, stealthily armed with a home-made bow and arrow, in search of prey that was singularly uncooperative or non-existent. In my imagination, I would go canoeing down to the mouth of the Margaret River, some 30 kilometres from our property. But this feat remained unrealized. In reality, it was quite unfeasible, as the river flowed too swiftly and was full of snags and sunken trees in winter, while in summer it was no more than a series of unconnected pools separated by dense ti-tree thickets.

The Margaret River, where it formed the southern border of the Burton farm — the site of swimming and marron-fishing excursions, and of Ruby's 'sink or swim' adventure (see Chapter 4).

The other river diversion was swimming. We learned to swim in the cold, fresh water of the pools into which the river subsided during summertime. There was no swimming in winter, as the swift flow of water made the river unsafe. In a particular pool with a gradually sloping bed we learned, without instruction, to dog paddle. At first, we made sure that our hands and knees could touch the bottom, keeping our heads above water. Soon we found that even when we ventured out a little further, we could support ourselves by thrashing around. The slope of the river bed was so gradual that even at the end of a furious burst of largely wasted energy, we could stand upright with our feet firmly planted on the bottom. As we became more confident, we were able to emulate the crawl, overarm and breaststroke of the more experienced swimmers and found ourselves at home in the deeper waters of the pool, jumping in or diving from the fallen dead trees on the river banks. We had plenty of self-assurance and later could readily identify with the happy, carefree natives that were often seen in travel films, splashing about in their tropical aquatic paradise. Except for the presence of one or two older children, we were for the most part unsupervised, and in retrospect it is surprising that there were no tragedies.

The one great drawback was the presence of leeches, which abounded in the river. These objectionable creatures attached themselves to our bodies and would no doubt have deterred most adults from entering the water. But then they were accepted as the price of a day's pleasure, and held no horrors for us. We were adept at counter-measures to ward them off, being on continual alert for their presence on our bodies and also keeping a close watch on the backs of other swimmers. The secret was to catch the slimy creature before it became fixed and drew blood. At this stage, it was easy to dislodge, and every one captured in this way—and they were always killed—was one less in the pool. If by chance one did become firmly attached, we removed it by the application of heat from a freshly extinguished match. A box of matches was usually on hand for this purpose. The smaller children were apprehensive of the leeches at first, but the obvious enjoyment of the older swimmers and their matter-of-fact attitude to the problem soon overcame these fears.

Nature's manifestations are not always pleasant, and leeches were by no means the only pest we had to contend with. The most common, and the most tormenting, were flies and ants. Ordinary houseflies could not be avoided, inside or outside the house. They dropped into one's food and drink, and swarmed on one's back. It was quite common for people to walk along carrying a small tree branch, to use — usually without much success — to swish away the flies from their head and back. The fly's breeding habits were obscure, but with animal droppings everywhere, there was no impediment to its life-cycle.

Not being able to eradicate them, settlers had to adopt the best protective measures possible. There were no fly-proof screens on doors and windows, and so the house was kept closed when the flies were most active. Fly-papers were hung from ceilings and over windows, to act as traps. These were small cardboard rolls containing sticky paper that pulled out into a concertina-like spiral, trapping any fly that alighted on it. A small hand-spray filled with insecticide was always at the ready for squirting persistent intruders and, hopefully, dissuading others. Food had to be carefully covered and stored. Items such as milk, sugar and jam were always protected by covers that my mother made from cheesecloth and weighted with beads.

Besides the houseflies there were blowflies, which had a nasty habit of laying their eggs in food. If undetected, the eggs would hatch into a revolting mass of maggots, which tended to put one off that type of food for some time. Fortunately, these persistent creatures usually came singly and made their presence felt by a loud buzzing sound that enabled the offender to be dealt with before it could do any harm.

A more silent intruder was the March fly which, as the name suggests, appeared around that month. The first one knew of its presence was a sharp sting on any exposed piece of flesh, usually an arm or a leg. This fly usually stayed where it had stung, making it easy to dispose of with a sharp, reflexive slap. The botfly was another revolting creature, with a large, bluish iridescent bulge at the back. It was never seen inside, its habitat being the pads of fresh manure lying around the paddocks.

The ant was just as ubiquitous. Fortunately, as our cottage was erected on stumps, ants found it difficult to get inside, but they were everywhere outside. The small, black, common ants scavenged widely. When one came upon a nest, built from thousands of tiny sticks and standing anything from 30 to 60 centimetres above ground level, one was struck by the quiet, orderly activity going on around it. Ants would be coming and going leisurely: some with small sticks or pieces of dried leaf to add to the nest; some alone, struggling with a dead insect, often larger than themselves; some working as a team, dragging an extra large insect or beetle presumably to add to the food store in the nest; some, their load delivered, moving away from the nest to search for another morsel of food or contribution to the nest. But disturb the nest with a stick and it became a heap of feverish activity. Ants poured out from within, hyperactive and ferociously attacking anything nearby. Such would be their numbers, and such the discomfort from their combined, feeble nipping, that one would be forced to retire, overwhelmed by the onslaught. They would immediately set to work repairing the damage, and within a remarkably short time the nest would be fully restored.

Not to be trifled with were the sergeant-ant and bull-ant. The former was two to three times larger than the common ant, a fiery red in colour, and aggressive in behaviour. The bull-ant was black and not quite as aggressive, unless provoked, but, like the sergeant-ant, it had a nasty sting and was to be avoided. They were usually found in the hard, gravelly ground rather than in sandy patches, their homes being tiny holes bored out of the stony soil.

There were also white-ants, as termites were called, which would attack the sapwood of any posts or timber in direct contact with the ground. However, with the tin capping on the stumps of the cottage, they rarely intruded inside. Their earthen mounds, often formed over the remains of a rotting log, were dotted throughout the bush.

Of course, the forces of nature were sometimes more serious. Bush fires were a rare but terrifying experience to everyone remotely connected with them. I recall only one fire involving fatalities: a fire near Margaret River in 1931, when two children of the Nillsson family were trapped by the advancing flames and lost their lives. The whole community was shaken by this tragedy and a large funeral was held at which scouts and guides attended in uniform to farewell their young scout companions. Although there were several controlled burns on neighbouring properties, we experienced only one menacing fire on ours. It was a near disaster for our hayshed with its stack of freshly gathered hay, which was to provide feed for the herd throughout the approaching summer months. My father had cleared about 5 hectares of land, and the debris — dead bushes and fallen trees — lay thick upon the ground, awaiting a favourable opportunity to fire it.

I do not know how the fire came to be lit, but the first we knew of it was when neighbours converged on our property and raised the alarm. Smoke billowing high into the air had alerted them. By then, the fire was beyond control. It raced with incredible speed towards the haystack, which was on the edge of the newly cleared area and directly in the path of the approaching inferno. Fortunately, our house was on the opposite side of the road in a cleared area, and appeared to be comparatively safe, although one can never be certain: with fierce eddies caused by the intense heat and with changing wind directions, the path of a fire is rarely predictable. All available hands hastened to provide water, carried to the scene in buckets, so that we could soak bags and sacking for beating out the flames if they approached the haystack. Further supplies of sacks were soaked in the river and provided close at hand. Neighbours helped to start a backburn, to exhaust the fuel in the path of the approaching flames.

Several people were deployed in preventing the fire spreading to adjacent paddocks, thus preserving what little feed was still left, and, of greater importance, in extinguishing any fires that attacked fence posts on the perimeter of the burning area. The paddocks between the fire and the creek were alive with frogs and toads that had migrated away from the inundated creek bed during the winter and had not yet returned to their summer quarters. Smooth skinned frogs, horny toads, frogs with warts, green ones, black ones, frogs in multi-coloured, iridescent hues — all hopped and collided with one another, oblivious of other dangers in their eagerness to scuttle to the safety of the creek.

The fire increased in ferocity, generating its own local whirlwinds, crackling loudly and rising to a roar as it progressed. The combined heat of the day and the fire seared eucalypts, releasing the rich loads of oil stored in their green leaves. The flames progressed not only at ground level but swirled from treetop to treetop, fuelled by oil evaporating from the super-heated leaves. Fortunately, the back-burning and a cleared space between the tinder-dry undergrowth and the haystack enabled the fire-fighters to retain control of the situation in the vicinity of the haystack. The direction of the feeble breeze was away from the stack. Except for an occasional burst of sparks from an eddy generated by the ferocity of the fire itself, there were no uncontrollable showers of sparks such as would have occurred if the wind had been blowing in the opposite direction. Where the advancing fire met the backburn, there was a large, dead tree with dry bark still adhering to its trunk and branches. The fierce flames spiralled up the tree, assisted by an updraft of air, and soon it was ablaze. It burned for three days and nights, and a continual watch had to be maintained to ensure that if the wind changed direction any free-flying sparks would not ignite the haystack. The smouldering fires in the junctions of the branches finally exhausted themselves, sometimes with a spectacular display of fireworks as a burnt branch came crashing to the ground. In the end, the haystack was not harmed, much to the relief of my father, who had had visions of starving cattle during the long summer ahead. Others were not so fortunate, and the distress we might have suffered was brought home to us one summer when a near neigh-bour lost a whole season's harvest through a haystack fire.

Such were the joys, the fears and the inconveniences of nature. The hazards, usually viewed with apprehension by city-dwellers, we took in our stride. The joys were relished and exploited to the full. Memories of them in later years make us sometimes regret, to paraphrase Shelley, 'that the mists of familiarity often obscure for us the wonder'.

Chapter Nine

Walking Off

THE ULTIMATE FAILURE OF THE GROUP SETTLEMENT SCHEME is no reflection on the magnificence of the vision from which it sprang or on those who came to give that vision life. No one, however far-sighted, could have predicted the conditions that caused it to fail. There is a tendency to blame either the originators of the scheme or the inexperience of the men and women who pioneered it. But every new venture is fraught with unforeseen hazards, and greater experience of farming and exposure to Australian conditions would only have made the final agonies less prolonged. The inexperienced tended to cling more tenaciously to their holdings, either through absence of an alternative or because of an inextinguishable flicker of hope that things would in the end improve. It was not, in the main, the quality of the manpower that caused the venture to fail, for on the whole the settlers toiled long and hard. It was the unforeseen and unforeseeable impact of the Great Depression and, in some areas, the unknown deficiencies of the soil. These deficiencies made farming almost impossible until the discovery, in the latter part of the 1930s, of the importance of trace elements. The financial cost of the scheme to the governments of the time was high enough, but the cost in human terms—the withering of the spirit caused by the journey from hope to despair and, in many cases, to desperation—is something that can only be understood by those who experienced it.

The outcome of the Group Settlement experiment was apparent long before the Depression, the full force of which was not felt by the settlers until 1931. By that year, the price of butterfat had plummeted to less than half of the value on which the economics of the scheme were based. The State treasury had no funds. State assistance had ceased when the blocks were valued and declared self-sufficient, which, in many cases, was done prematurely. From that time forward, instead of the settler receiving assistance from the State, interest on the assessed capital value was deducted from cream cheques every three months, and supervising foremen were withdrawn. I recall that one month, after deduction of interest, my father received a cheque for $2 to keep the family of five until the next monthly cheque was received. There were widespread recriminations at all levels. As one researcher has written, 'Those who had earlier been called "splendid people" had now become "poor citizens".* This unfair apportionment of blame by desperate politicians only served further to discourage and embitter settlers who now felt themselves completely abandoned.

The meagre cash reserves that my parents had brought out with them — intended for the return passage to England — including the small amounts held in bank accounts in the children's names, were exhausted. We were by any standards poor, but the strange thing was that we children hardly noticed it. This was probably because although our fare was frugal, we never went hungry. Besides, everyone else in the district was in the same position, so there were no sharp contrasts by which to judge one's condition. For the adults, however, the effects were devastating, and the more distressing because they were undeserved. For some, the experience broke their spirit and ruined their lives. For others, particularly the children, it tempered their characters as fire tempers steel, preparing them for the rigours of a war that was still ten years ahead and for the dangers and opportunities of the postwar world.

My father did not know which way to turn and felt that he had let the family down. The situation wore down my mother's health, and she developed a duodenal ulcer. She suffered for months, the ulcer finally reaching life-threatening proportions. After diagnosis and palliative treatment at the Margaret River hospital, she was

---

* I.L. Hunt, 'A History of Group Settlement in the South West of W.A.', MA thesis, University of Western Australia, 1957.

evacuated to Perth for surgery and was carried off the train on a stretcher after collapsing en route.

My father accompanied her to Perth, leaving me to milk the cows and keep the farm going. I had just turned thirteen, and was excused from school attendance because of the situation. I carried on alone, with advice from helpful neighbours, until my father's return a month later, after my mother's name had been removed from the danger list and she was starting to recover. She was advised against returning to the country, so my father came back to finalize affairs, probably with some sense of relief that the matter had been taken out of his hands. He did not personally have to make the decision to abandon the results of over five years' labour, which would have been a tacit admission of failure. In fact, the circumstances of the enforced decision had their advantages, as there was no assurance of government assistance if one simply walked off the block. Unemployment relief was frequently denied or delayed if a settler left the scheme of his own accord. This led many settlers to 'arrange' to be dismissed by a sympathetic foreman so that they could access desperately needed relief from the State.

There were many things for my father to attend to before we left. After the fashion of the times, he took pride in the fact that with his last cream cheque, he was able to settle all his outstanding debts to tradespeople.

One sad duty was the disposal of our dog, Spot, who, with his withered leg and long attachment to the family, would have been unlikely to settle down in a new home. He disappeared on the evening of our last day. The prospect of our journey to the city and the forthcoming reunion with my mother in Perth was uppermost in my mind, but I recall my father coming into the room late that evening with a good family friend whose wife, it is obvious with hindsight, had been keeping us children occupied with card games. I remember his solemn and downcast look and noted the significant exchange of glances between the adults. It was not until some time later that I connected the episode with the exit of Spot from our lives and realized what a difficult task it must have been for my father to have to put down such a faithful friend.

And so, in October 1932, in the midst of the Depression, we walked off the block on which so much effort had been expended. My father knew that he faced a daunting future, but he left with his head held high, knowing that he had done his best.

The lines from Byron's 'English Bards and Scotch Reviewers' used as the epigraph to this book are enigmatically appropriate to its story:

> Who conquers me shall find a stubborn foe.

Do these words represent the challenge thrown down by the stubborn bushland, resisting the intrusion of man with a relentless tendency to revert, over time, to something approaching its original condition, or, if left long enough, to completely obliterate all signs of man's habitation? Or do they apply more aptly to those settler-pioneers who, in the third decade of the twentieth century, struggled tenaciously to overcome the nearly overwhelming odds that nature and the economic system had stacked against them? Whichever the reader chooses, there is something dramatic in the story of the group settlers; something heroic; something that, despite its tragic elements, I would not have missed.

The author and his family, at the unveiling of a memorial plaque to pioneers of the Osmington and Airdale districts, during Australia's bicentennial year, 1988.
Left to right: The author, his son Stuart, daughter-in-law Rose, sisters Margery and Mary Front: Grandchildren Alistair, Hamish and Jessica

Epilogue

SEVERAL PREVIEWERS OF THIS NARRATIVE have commented that its ending leaves the reader wondering about the subsequent fortunes of the members of my family. However, I feel that my story does properly end at this point. It was never primarily intended to be biographical. The intention was to portray a collective rather than an individual experience; to convey through the recounting of my own personal recollections a common experience that was the lot not only of my own family but of hundreds of others. Most of these have taken their stories with them into silence, but others, children of the original pioneers, hold nostalgic memories of those harsh days in the South West.

As a concession to those whose curiosity is still unsatisfied, I can say that my parents lived for over forty years after the events in the narrative and died content in the knowledge that their principal purpose in migrating to Australia, to give their children opportunities not available in England, had been achieved. My father was senile in his latter years. My mother, her faculties clear to the end and her faith in her God unshaken, dictated her epitaph to me a few days before her death. 'Write', she said, 'In Heavenly Love Abiding'.

Budget for a Family of Four

Income $12 per fortnight

	$
Sickness and accident fund (compulsory)	0.20
Food and lighting	8.50
Clothing	3.30
Total	12.00

Recommended store order (two weeks' supply)

	$
25 kilograms flour	0.70
2.5 kilograms wheatmeal	0.12
1 kilogram split peas	0.07
0.75 kilogram lentils	0.15
3 kilograms harvest beans	0.17
1 bag oatmeal	0.20
1.5 kilograms rice, sago, pearl barley, tapioca or macaroni	0.10
6 kilograms sugar	0.50
2 tins treacle	0.15
4 tins jam	0.30
Eggs	0.20
1 tin meat 11c, 3 tins fish 30c	0.41
1 tin dried milk	0.15
1 tin Nestles milk	0.08
1 kilogram butter	0.40
1 kilogram dripping	0.15
0.5 kilogram lard	0.09
1 big bar soap, 1 piece blue	0.20
0.25 kilogram borax, 0.5 kilogram washing soda	0.04

Condiments	0.30
4 kilograms mutton 45c, corned meat 45c	0.90
6 kilograms hindquarter	0.70
14 kilograms potatoes	0.40
1 kilogram dried apples	0.25
1 kilogram prunes	0.20
1 tin custard powder	0.12
0.5 kilogram cheese	0.15
0.25 kilogram cocoa 7c, 1 kilogram tea 30c	0.37
1 tin kerosene 20 litres (two months' supply)	0.21
1 packet matches 6c, tobacco 40c	0.46
0.5 kilogram bacon	0.16
0.5 kilogram dates, currants or raisins	0.10
Total	8.50

(*Source: Battye Library*)
Note: Converted to metrics

SCHEDULE OF OCCUPANTS OF GROUP 85 BLOCKS, 1927–32

Location No.	Occupants
2291	A. Thorne
2292	B.C. Burton
2293	J. Guyan (c. 1926–28) L.G.F. Spry (from 1928; prior to moving to Location 2293, Mr Spry had occupied Location 2890)
2295	A. Clark
2298	W.A. Howarth (to c. 1928) W. Alderson (from c. 1928)
2300	F.C. Reid (to c. 1928) J.O. Turnbull (c. 1928–30; brother-in-law of W. Alderson) W. Thomas (from c. 1930)
2888	H. Pickering
2889	C.E. (Tom) Barnfield (c. 1932 Mr Barnfield moved to Location 2289 on Group 84 [Airdale])
2890	L.G.F. Spry Sale A. McCabe
2891	Dale T. McCabe (brother of A. McCabe)

Location No.	Occupants
2930	A.J. Neal
2932	E.W. Cooper
2933	W. Piggott (to c. 1929) F. George (from c. 1930)
2935	B.C. Burton (1927) A. Jones (to c. 1930) G. Franklin (c. 1931–32)

OCCUPIED BLOCKS ON GROUP 85, 1927–32

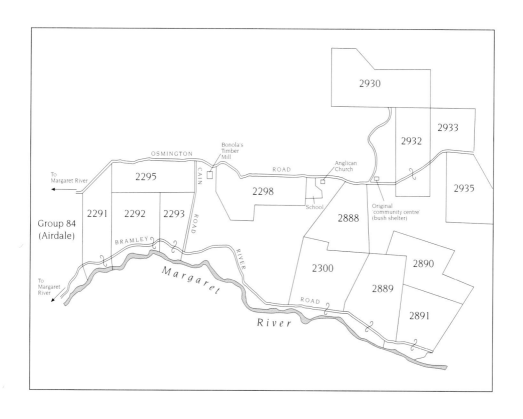

FURTHER READING –
GROUP SETTLEMENT

Historical Accounts

Blond, P.E.M., *A Tribute to the Group Settlers*, Nedlands: University of Western Australia Press, 1987.

Cresswell, G.J., *The Light of Leeuwin*, Margaret River: Augusta-Margaret River History Group, [1990?].

Gabbedy, J.P., *Group Settlement* (2 vols), Nedlands: University of Western Australia Press, 1988.

Anecdotal Accounts

Bunbury, B., *Reading Labels on Jam Tins: Living through Difficult Times*, Fremantle: Fremantle Arts Centre Press, 1993.

French, J., *Tale of a Groupie's Son: 89 West Pemberton*, Augusta: J. French, 1989.

McRobb, M., *The Lean Years*, Bunbury: South West Printing and Publishing Company, [1984?].

Payne, J.D., *Over the Bridge*, Margaret River: J. Payne, 1987.

References in the Battye Library

'Group Settlement in W.A.' (PR1216).

W.B. Amery, 'Report on the Group Settlements in W.A.' (325.941).

Instructions issued by J. Mitchell (Minister for Lands) (OH297).

W. Hart, 'A Battle for Existence' (QB/WHI).

T.S. Grosser, 'The Lure of the Golden West' (266.3).

'Report of Royal Commission on Group Settlement' (Q328.9414).

'Group Settlement Conditions' (2673A).

'Group Settlement Schooling' (PR5349/1).

'They Laboured with their Hands' (PR5349/18).

T.W. Doyle, 'Some Impressions of the Group Settlement Scheme in Western Australia' (Q333.76).

I.L. Hunt, 'A History of Group Settlement in the South West of W.A.', MA thesis, University of Western Australia, 1957 (Q333.7).